"I found Sr. Kathleen's book extraordinarily stimulating. I sat here in my offic_ _____ _____ _____ ...ntary students doing the playlets in a number of settings; in class, before a group of other students, and as part of a children's Liturgy of the Word. I grew excited thinking how easy it would be to stage and prepare the students for these experiences. I especially liked the ease and brevity of each play. This allows plenty of room for children to stretch their own imaginations.

"The indices at the end of the book are very helpful, both for themes and for choosing the appropriate Sunday Gospel. This is important for busy catechists who are also preparing a children's Liturgy of the Word with little time to research topics or dates. The plays are staged so simply that even the most impoverished parish program should be able to perform them e_ ___ ____ ___ _____ ____ __ ___ _____ _ *__1g Out the Gospels to every school and religious education pr_

> Patrick R. Guentert
> Director of Catechetical Services
> Diocese of Lexington

"*Acting Out the Gospels* presents an exciting way to bring the Scripture to life in catechetical classrooms. It offers busy DREs and catechists a ready resource for diversifying the presentation of the Scripture stories. This is an exciting teaching tool that makes 'hands on' learning about Scripture easy"

> Frank Lucido, Ed.D.
> Secretary for Education/Director of Religious Education
> Diocese of Corpus Christi

"Classroom teachers who often have limited time and resources will be able to use this material easily. These playlets are all between one and two pages in length and are presented in large type. They span Jesus' life from the infancy narratives through his public life, and on through the passion stories. Included with the scripts are a short exegesis, two or three discussion questions, and simple tips for the 'director.' There is an index of themes and a chart arranging the readings according to the lectionary year."

> Rev. Susan M. Clark
> *The Living Church*

"These plays fit in well with most religion textbooks. They can stand on their own as an effective introduction to a particular theme or incident, and can be used within the context of a lesson or liturgy. The helpful directions list the cast and props needed, themes, comments on production, and points for discussion with students following the performance. The book also contains a chart that relates each Gospel event to an applicable Sunday or feast day, making it useful for planning student liturgies."

> *Doctrine and Life*

"The best feature of this book are the guidelines for directing these playlets, including lists of props and characters, as well as guidelines for leading discussions designed to make the most of the plays' themes. The plays in this book would be appropriately performed in church school classes or on special occasions for the entire congregation. I highly recommend it for church libraries."

> Suellen S. Briggs
> *Church & Synagogue Libraries*

"This is another of Sr. Kathleen's aids for the teaching and understanding of Sacred Scripture. Most valuable is a detailed description of the cast of characters, plus staging and background material to help integrate each episode into the larger story of Jesus' life."

> Msgr. Charles Diviney
> *The Tablet*

ACTING OUT
The Gospels

40 Five-Minute Plays
for Education and Worship

Mary Kathleen Glavich, SND

XXIII

TWENTY-THIRD PUBLICATIONS
Mystic, CT 06355

Acknowledgments

I am grateful to
Sister Mary Joell Overman, S.N.D., Sister Rita Mary Harwood, S.N.D.,
Sister Mary Margaret Hess, S.N.D., and to the many other Sisters in my community
who have encouraged and supported me
in my writing ministry.
My appreciation, too, to the kind and helpful personnel at
Twenty-Third Publications who have made this book a reality.

Dedication

To the Most Reverend Anthony M. Pilla, Bishop of Cleveland,
in gratitude for his wholehearted and courageous leadership

The Gospel passages contained herein are from the New Revised Standard Version of the Bible, copyright © 1989, by the Division of Christian Education of the National Council of Churches of Christ in the U.S.A. All rights reserved.

Twenty-Third Publications
185 Willow Street
P.O. Box 180
Mystic, CT 06355
(860) 536-2611
(800) 321-0411

Table of Contents

Introduction

Acting Out the Gospels is a companion to *Acting Out the Miracles and Parables: 52 Five-Minute Plays for Education and Worship.* It contains forty events from the gospel accounts of the life of Jesus (other than miracles and parables) in play form. The playlets can be incorporated into lessons on related topics. They are an alternative to having the students read the textbook, read the Bible, or produce their own plays. Certainly student-created plays are interesting, fun, and effective learning activities. But writing plays consumes much class time, and sometimes the students' plays are so original that they can hardly be identified as gospel stories! The ready-made plays in this book are based directly on Scripture.

These brief plays can be used in a lesson as
- *a lively introduction,*
- *a method of developing a Bible story,*
- *a review activity,*
- *a culminating activity, or*
- *a lead-in to a prayer experience.*

They can be presented
- *for another class or other group,*
- *as part of a program for parents and other guests, or*
- *within a liturgical or paraliturgical service.*

The playlets are adaptable to any grade level for several reasons. The gospel stories themselves are simple and so is their vocabulary. Most of them are familiar. Furthermore, the lessons of the basic religion text provide the necessary preparation and follow-up that make the playlets consonant with the students' developmental stage.

Most of the wording of the playlets is based on the *New Revised Standard Version of the Bible.* Those playlets for events that appear in more than one gospel account are a blend of those accounts. Where dialogue is described in the Scriptures or merely implied, it has been supplied.

Each playlet in this book is on a separate page(s) so that copies can be easily duplicated for the actors and others involved in staging the playlets. Names marked + under "Cast" in the stage directions can be adjusted to the size of the class to allow as many students as possible to participate.

Catechists, especially novice producers and directors, should not miss "Tips for Putting on Playlets" on page 2. The ten suggestions there are important for smooth performances that are rewarding for all.

Two features in the stage directions help catechists plan when each playlet would be most appropriate. The first is a chart on page 117 of those Sunday or feastday gospels in each liturgical cycle that have a corresponding play in this book. This is for ease in preparing for Sunday or feastday liturgies that may be enhanced by a playlet. The second feature is a topical index to assist in correlating the plays in this book with the year's curriculum.

The stage directions that precede each play prepare catechists to use the playlets. Each gospel event is explained briefly under "Background Notes." These notes clarify what happened, supply background information, and indicate the event's significance. In addition, discussion questions for before and after the performance are suggested for each play. Some of these questions focus on the main message of the Scripture passage. Others are intended to investigate concepts that students might find puzzling or overlook. Most important, some points lead the students to relate the events to themselves and their world. The stage directions also suggest a prayer activity that can be carried out at the end of the play.

Acting Out the Gospels should be a help to all catechists who regard variety and student involvement as essential ingredients of a good lesson. Its ready-made playlets will enable us to teach creatively without undue time spent preparing plays. In addition, our students will encounter the Scriptures and Jesus in an enjoyable way: through an experience they will remember more than reading a page in a book.

Tips for Putting on Playlets

1. Make a copy of the playlet for each participant who has a speaking part or a major role. Write their names on the copies and highlight, or have the students highlight, their parts, including stage directions.

2. Make an identification sign, headband, or sandwich board for each character.

3. Allow as many students as possible to participate in the playlet. Cast names marked + on the stage directions can be adjusted to the size of your class.

4. Prepare the props that are suggested for some playlets. Printed signs indicating the setting are also helpful, particularly if the location changes during the play. Pictures of scenery can be drawn on the blackboard. If possible, have the students wear costumes.

5. List the characters on the board so that students can sign for parts before class. They might have time to practice and even memorize their lines.

6. Arrange to have the actors rehearse together during class while the rest of the students are engaged in another activity. A teacher aide might take the group to another room for practice.

7. Encourage the participants to…
   look up from their scripts as much as possible,
   speak so as to be heard and understood,
   avoid having their backs to the audience,
   use expression in interpreting their lines, and
   be creative in adding movements and gestures.

8. Before the playlet begins, have the characters introduce themselves to the audience, especially if they are not wearing identification.

9. Compliment the group or individuals for a job well done. You might have the class evaluate their performance.

10. Make sure that each student has a speaking role at some time and is not always just a member of the crowd.

Caution: Avoid putting on a playlet only for the sake of putting on a playlet. With no proper introduction or follow-up, a playlet is largely a waste of time instead of a meaningful educational experience.

The Infancy Narratives

Leader's Guide

Background Notes:
Elizabeth and Zechariah were righteous people who were childless like Abraham and Sarah. While Zechariah is praying, God reveals startling news to him. Zechariah and Elizabeth will have a son who will be great in God's sight.

The day John's birth was announced was special for Zechariah. Out of eight hundred priests in his division, he was chosen by lot to offer incense that day in the Holy Place of the Temple. The many people present suggest that he was doing this during the evening hours. Gabriel appears and says, "Do not be afraid," to Zechariah. This is just what Gabriel will say to Mary six months later. These words often preface a redemptive act of God. Gabriel's words to Zechariah follow the formula for a birth announcement commonly used in Scripture. The angel foretells that John will be a Nazarite dedicated to God as Samson was. God will empower him to be the forerunner of Jesus and help bring about the messianic age. Like Elijah, he will announce the Lord. He will be a great prophet. Zechariah is left speechless by the good news—either because he lacked faith or because he was overcome by joy.

Times for Use: Advent, lessons on the infancy narratives, John the Baptist, openness to God, faith.

CAST   PROPS

CAST	PROPS
Narrator	**Table for altar**
Zechariah	**Incense**
Angel Gabriel	
Persons 1, 2, 3+	

QUESTIONS FOR CHILDREN

Before the play: What are angels? What is their role? What angels do you know of? When is a good time to pray to your guardian angel?

After the play: How is this event similar to the announcement of Jesus' birth? How is it different? What other times has God done the impossible—in the life of Jesus? In your life? How else does God speak to us besides through angels?

CLASS PRAYER:

(Tell the students to think of a special prayer intention. It can be something personal or something as broad as world peace.)

Zechariah and Elizabeth were faithful to God. They never stopped relying on God for help. They never stopped praying. Let us pray to be like them.

O God, you heard the prayers of Zechariah and Elizabeth and gave them a son. This was a miracle because they were so old. Give me the grace to trust you to do miracles for me, too. Give me strong faith so that in times of need I turn to you for help. Then let me keep praying even though it seems you are not listening. I believe that you can do the impossible. Please surprise me, especially by…

The Announcement of John's Birth

(Zechariah kneels before table with incense. Persons 1, 2, 3 kneel praying at a distance.)

Narrator   Zechariah was a priest. He and his wife Elizabeth were good, holy people. They were very old and never had any children. One day Zechariah was chosen by lot to burn incense in the Temple. People prayed outside.

(Angel Gabriel enters and stands at right of altar. Zechariah gasps, trembles, and stands with hands up.)

Angel   Do not be afraid, Zechariah, because your prayer has been heard. Your wife Elizabeth will bear you a son, and you will name him John. You will have joy and gladness, and many people will rejoice at his birth, for he will be great in the sight of the Lord. He must never drink wine or strong drink. Even before his birth he will be filled with the Holy Spirit. He will turn many people of Israel to the Lord their God. He will make a people ready for the Lord.

Zechariah   How will I know this is so? For I am an old man, and my wife is an old woman.

Angel   I am Gabriel, who stand before God. I was sent to announce to you this good news. But now, because you did not believe my words, (shaking finger at Zechariah) you will be unable to talk until the day these things take place. (Angel exits.)

Person 1   What's taking Zechariah so long? He should be finished by now.

Person 2   Maybe he's ill. He's pretty old.

(Zechariah rises and walks slowly in a daze toward the people.)

Person 1   Here he comes.

(Persons 1, 2 rise.)

(Zechariah gestures to the place he left and to his mouth. He points to heaven.)

Person 3   Why doesn't he speak?

Person 2   I think he's had a vision.

Narrator   Zechariah learned to trust God's messages. The angel's words came true. Zechariah and Elizabeth had a son known as John the Baptist.

Leader's Guide

Background Notes:

The announcement of the immediate coming of the Messiah was made to Mary, a virgin in Nazareth. Although Nazareth was an insignificant town scorned by Palestinians, it would be the hometown of the Savior of the world. Mary would have a son conceived miraculously by the overshadowing of the Holy Spirit. This conception surpasses the conception of John, whose parents conceived him naturally, although they were advanced in age.

The angel Gabriel greets Mary with words of great praise. He discloses that God has chosen her to bear a son who is the Son of God. She is to name him Jesus, which means "God saves." The words Gabriel used to describe Mary's son, such as "Son of the Most High," are those that signify God's redeeming presence in the Old Testament. Mary is espoused to Joseph, who is of the family of David. Because Joseph would be Jesus' legal father, it is through him, not Mary, that Jesus would trace his lineage.

Mary accepts God's will for her and merits her name, which in Hebrew means "exalted one." In trust and obedience she agrees to be a virgin-mother, the mother of the Savior. She stands as a model for all who are called to bring forth Christ into the world and to further his kingdom.

Times for Use: Feasts of Mary, Advent, lessons on the infancy narratives, obedience, openness to God, Mary, the identity of Jesus, the Holy Spirit.

CAST

Narrator
Gabriel
Mary

QUESTIONS FOR CHILDREN

Before the play: Why is it amazing that God became a human being? Why do you think God chose Mary to be the mother of Jesus? Why was being God's Mother a difficult thing for Mary to do? Why did she agree to do it?

After the play: What were some privileges God gave Mary because she is the Mother of God? How is Mary your mother too? How can you show devotion to Mary? What is the best way?

CLASS PRAYER:

Pray the Angelus together. Explain that it was a custom to pray the Angelus in honor of the incarnation three times a day: at morning, noon, and evening. Church bells rang at these times to remind Christians to pray the Angelus.

The Angelus

The angel of the Lord declared unto Mary
And she conceived of the Holy Spirit.

Hail Mary…

Behold the handmaid of the Lord.
Be it done to me according to your word.

Hail Mary…

And the Word was made flesh
And dwelt among us.

Hail Mary…

Pray for us, O holy Mother of God
That we may be made worthy of the promises of Christ.

Let us pray.
Pour forth, we beseech you, O Lord, your grace into our hearts, that we to whom the incarnation of Christ, your Son was made known by the message of an angel, may by his passion and death be brought to the glory of his resurrection, through the same Christ our Lord. Amen.

The Annunciation

(Mary is walking on the stage.)

Narrator   The angel Gabriel was sent from God to a town of Galilee called Nazareth, to a virgin engaged to a man named Joseph, of the house of David. And the virgin's name was Mary.

(Gabriel enters and goes to Mary. Mary gasps and looks frightened.)

Gabriel   Hail, favored one! The Lord is with you.

(Mary puts her hand over her heart and tilts head, looking puzzled.)

Gabriel   (Raises hand) Do not be afraid, Mary, for you have found favor with God. And now, you will conceive in your womb and bear a son, and you will name him Jesus. He will be great and will be called Son of the Most High. The Lord God will give him the throne of his ancestor, David. He will rule over the house of Jacob forever, and of his kingdom there will be no end.

Mary   How can this be, since I have no relations with a man?

Gabriel   The Holy Spirit will come upon you, and the power of the Most High will overshadow you. Therefore the child to be born will be called holy, the Son of God. And now, your relative Elizabeth in her old age has also conceived a son. She who was called barren is now in her sixth month of pregnancy. For nothing will be impossible with God.

Mary   (bowing) Behold, I am the handmaid of the Lord. Let it be done to me according to your word.

(Gabriel exits.)

Narrator   Because Mary was open to doing God's will, she became the mother of God. Her son, Jesus, saved the world. We try to be like our mother Mary by always doing what God wants.

Leader's Guide

Background Notes:
Mary's union with God prompts her to selfless action. Hastening to assist her elderly relative, Elizabeth, she undertakes a journey of about ninety miles. When the two women meet, Elizabeth recognized the great blessing that has come to Mary. The baby in her womb leaps, a sign of messianic joy. It is Jesus who is the reason for John's greatness and mission in life. John is quickened with new life, the life of the Spirit. Tradition holds that at that moment John the Baptist was freed from sin.

Mary's hymn of praise is called the *Magnificat* from the Latin for the opening words. It is similar to Hannah's song (1 Samuel 2:1–10). The church prays the *Magnificat* every day in evening prayer. In this canticle, Mary reflects on her role as handmaid favored by God and Mary recalls the great themes of salvation history: the surprising reversals as God acts on behalf of the poor and needy. The rich and powerful are brought low, while the poor and humble are raised. Mary closes her song by proclaiming that God has kept the promise made to Abraham. Israel, a servant, has been favored.

Times for Use: Lessons on the infancy narratives, Mary, John the Baptist, service, the poor.

CAST   PROPS

Narrator   **Pot and Ladle or Broom**
Mary   **Two Chairs**
Elizabeth

QUESTIONS FOR CHILDREN

Before the play: Did someone ever do something special for you so that you knew God's love through that person? What were some hardships Mary experienced in going to visit Elizabeth? Why did she go?

After the play: What was the relationship between Jesus and John in salvation history? Why was Mary's *Magnificat* appropriate for the occasion? What are some hard things you have done to love and serve the members of your family? What could you do for them?

CLASS PRAYER

Pray the *Magnificat* in one of the following ways:
• Read it and have the students close their eyes and join in the prayer in their hearts.
• Invite them to listen to a musical setting of it, such as John Michael Talbot's "Holy Is Your Name."
• Show a transparency of it or distribute copies. Have the students pray all of it together or designate two sides and have them alternate verses.

The Magnificat

My soul magnifies the Lord,
  and my spirit rejoices in God my Savior,
for he has looked with favor on the lowliness of his servant.
  Surely, from now on all generations will call me blessed;
for the Mighty One has done great things for me,
  and holy is his name.
His mercy is for those who fear him
  from generation to generation.
He has shown strength with his arm;
  he has scattered the proud in the thoughts of their hearts.
He has brought down the powerful from their thrones,
  and lifted up the lowly;
he has filled the hungry with good things,
  and sent the rich away empty.
He has helped his servant Israel,
  in remembrance of his mercy,
according to the promise he made to our ancestors,
  to Abraham and to his descendants forever.

The Visitation

(Elizabeth is off to the side, stirring a pot or sweeping the floor. Two chairs are in the center of the stage.)

Narrator   After the angel Gabriel appeared to her, Mary traveled in haste to a town of Judah in the hill country. She was going to help her elderly relative Elizabeth, who was pregnant.

(Mary enters and goes quickly toward Elizabeth. She pretends to open a door and steps inside.)

Mary   Elizabeth, dear! How are you?

Elizabeth   (surprised) Ah? (Puts her hand on her stomach)…Mary!

(Mary and Elizabeth hug.)

Elizabeth   (excitedly) Blessed are you among women, and blessed is the fruit of your womb. And why does this happen to me, that the mother of my Lord comes to me? For as soon as I heard the sound of your greeting, the child in my womb leaped for joy. Blessed are you who believed that what was spoken to you by the Lord would be fulfilled.

Mary   My soul proclaims the greatness of the Lord.
My spirit rejoices in God my savior.
For he has looked with favor on his handmaid's lowliness.
Behold, from now on all ages will call me blessed.
The Mighty One has done great things for me,
and holy is his name.
His mercy is to those who fear him
from age to age.
He has shown might with his arm and
scattered the proud.
He has thrown down the powerful from their thrones
and lifted up the lowly.
He has filled the hungry with good things,
and sent the rich away empty.
He has helped his servant Israel,
remembering his mercy,
according to his promise to our fathers,
to Abraham and to his descendants forever.

Elizabeth   Zechariah will be home soon. He can't speak, you know, ever since he found out about our baby. He'll be glad to see you too! How long can you stay?

Mary   About three months.

Elizabeth   Wonderful! Now tell me about yourself and the great things the Lord has done for you.

(Mary and Elizabeth sit down.)

Narrator   Mary helped Elizabeth during the last months of her pregnancy. Then she returned home to prepare for her own child. We pray to be as generous and selfless as Mary was.

Leader's Guide

Background Notes:
John is not named after his father, as was the custom. He who is to be the messenger of God is named by God. When Zechariah affirms the name John, he regains the power of speech. Everyone is filled with wonder, and Zechariah praises God. The first part of his canticle is modeled on Jewish circumcision ceremonies. The second part links John to the Savior. It gives his identity in relation to Jesus. The hopes and promises of the Jewish forefathers will soon be fulfilled. The dayspring will dawn to save people from darkness. Zechariah's song is prayed every day in the morning praise of the Liturgy of the Hours, the official prayer of the church.

Times for Use: Advent, with lessons on the infancy narratives, John the Baptist.

CAST	PROPS
Narrator	Paper
Zechariah	Pencil
Elizabeth	Doll or Blanket for Baby
Persons 1, 2, 3+	

QUESTIONS FOR CHILDREN

Before the play: Do you know why you received your name? Who gave you your name? What does your name mean?

After the play: What was to be John's mission? When were you called by God and given a mission? What is your mission? What are some reasons you have for blessing the Lord as Zechariah did?

CLASS PRAYER

Pray this excerpt from the Canticle of Zechariah:

Canticle of Zechariah

Blessed be the Lord God of Israel,
  for he has looked favorably on his people and
    redeemed them.
He has raised up a mighty savior for us
  in the house of his servant David.
And you, child, will be called prophet of the Most
    High,
  for you will go before the Lord to prepare his ways,
to give knowledge of salvation to his people
  through the forgiveness of their sins.
By the tender mercy of our God,
  the dawn from on high will break upon us
to give light to those who sit in darkness and in the
    shadow of death,
to guide our feet into the way of peace.

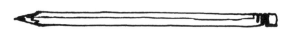

The Birth of John

LUKE 1:57–80

Narrator   When Elizabeth and her husband Zechariah were very old, she bore a son. Now she was no longer ashamed for being childless, and she thanked God. Eight days after her son was born, neighbors and relatives came for a Jewish celebration when the baby would be named.

(Zechariah, Elizabeth carrying a baby, and Persons 1, 2, 3 enter.)

Person 1   Let's name him Zechariah.

Person 2   Yes, he should be named after his father.

Elizabeth   No, he is to be called John.

Person 3   But none of your relatives has this name.

(Persons 1, 2, 3 turn to Zechariah, point to baby, and raise their hands questioningly.)

(Zechariah motions as if writing and extends his hand. Person 2 brings pencil and paper. Zechariah writes. Person 1 looks over his shoulder.)

Person 1   He wrote, "John is his name."

Person 3   I don't believe it. How strange.

Zechariah   Blessed be God!

Person 2   (excitedly) He can speak now!

Person 1   What can this mean?

Person 3   Let's get out of here.

Person 2   What will this child be?

Zechariah   (takes baby from Elizabeth)
Blessed be the Lord God of Israel,
for he has looked favorably on his people and redeemed them.
He has raised up a mighty savior for us
in the house of his servant David.
(holding up baby) And you, child, will be called prophet of the Most High,

for you will go before the Lord to prepare his ways,
to give knowledge of salvation to his people
through the forgiveness of their sins.
By the tender mercy of our God,
the dawn from on high will break upon us
to give light to those who sit in darkness and in the shadow of death,
to guide our feet into the way of peace.

Narrator The child of Zechariah and Elizabeth was John the Baptist, the great prophet who prepared the people for Jesus. Let us always be prepared to welcome Jesus.

Leader's Guide

Background Notes:
In the Scriptures, the birth of the Savior is told in the context of the Roman empire. Mary and Joseph are good citizens responding to a call for a worldwide census. People must return to their own towns to register. Because Joseph is of the House of David, he must return to Bethlehem, about ninety miles from Nazareth. Joseph finds shelter and privacy in a room where people kept livestock. The stable was probably a cave, the back room of a house. There Mary gives birth to Jesus. She wraps him in swaddling clothes, long strips that Palestinians used so that their children would grow straight and strong. The newborn boy, who would someday be the bread of life, is placed in a manger, a feeding trough. He is Mary's firstborn, the first of many others—his future followers.

Angels announce to shepherds the good news of the child's birth. Shepherds were poor people whose job was that of the patriarchs: to guard and guide. In their proclamation, the angels refer to Jesus as Savior, Messiah, and Lord. The news is especially exciting for the shepherds because the Messiah has appeared in humble surroundings, like one of them.

Times for Use: Christmas, lessons on the infancy narratives, identity of Jesus, Mary, the good news, obedience to law, poverty.

QUESTIONS FOR CHILDREN

Before the play: How does your family celebrate Christmas? Why is this a great feast? Who are some people in the Christmas story?

After the play: Why do you think God chose to be born in a stable? How does Jesus come to us today? How can we make room for Jesus in our lives?

CLASS PRAYER

Gather the students around the manger. Pray or sing the Glory to God (Gloria) which begins with the prayer of the angels: "Glory to God in the highest and peace to his people on earth," or sing a religious Christmas carol such as "Silent Night," "O Come, All Ye Faithful," or "Hark the Herald Angels Sing."

CAST   PROPS

Narrator
Mary
Joseph
Innkeeper
Angel 1
Angels+
Shepherd 1
Shepherd 2+

The Birth of Jesus

LUKE 2:1–20

(Shepherds are on one side of the stage. Half are sleeping. Innkeeper is on other side, writing on a scroll.)

Narrator   In those days a decree went out from Emperor Augustus that the whole world should be registered. This was the first census, when Quirinius was governor of Syria. So all went to their own towns to be registered. And Joseph also went from the town of Nazareth in Galilee to Judea, to the city of David called Bethlehem, because he was of the house and family of David. He went to be registered with Mary, to whom he was engaged and who was expecting a child.

(Mary and Joseph enter, walking slowly. They stop at "door" and Joseph knocks. Innkeeper goes to door.)

Innkeeper   Yes?

Joseph   Would you have room for two more, my wife and me?

Innkeeper   Sorry, but the house is filled.

Joseph   We'd appreciate even a small space. My wife is expecting any day now.

Innkeeper   (shaking head) Sorry. Wish I could help. Wait. There's the stable in the back.

Joseph   That would be fine.

Innkeeper   Come with me.

(Mary and Joseph go to center of stage with the Innkeeper.
Joseph helps Mary to a chair.)

Joseph   (to Innkeeper) Thank you, sir.

Innkeeper   Good night. (Exits.)

Mary   It's almost time, Joseph.

(While Narrator speaks, Joseph, with his back to the audience, takes the doll and cloths from the basket. He gives them to Mary. She wraps the doll in the cloths and sets it in the manger.)

Narrator   While they were there, the time came for Mary to have her child, and she gave birth to her firstborn son. She wrapped him in swaddling clothes and laid him in a manger.

(Angel 1 enters and stands before the Shepherds. Shepherds gasp and shield their faces. The sleeping ones awake and rub their eyes.)

Angel 1   Do not be afraid. Behold, I bring you good news of great joy for all the people. For today in the city of David a savior has been born for you who is Messiah, the Lord. This will be a sign for you: You will find an infant wrapped in swaddling clothes and lying in a manger.

(Angels enter and join Angel 1.)

Angels   Glory to God in the highest and on earth peace to those whom he favors. (Exit.)

Shepherd 1   (to Shepherd 2) Let us go now to Bethlehem and see this thing that has taken place, which the Lord has made known to us.

(Shepherds run to Mary and Joseph.)

Shepherd 2   (to Mary and Joseph) We have come to see the infant. We were watching our flocks, and angels appeared and told us that a savior was born in Bethlehem. They said we would find him in a manger.

(Mary and Joseph gesture to manger. Shepherds kneel around it.)

Joseph   (to Mary) What an amazing story! (Mary smiles and nods.)

(Shepherds rise.)

Shepherd 1   Well, we'd better go back to our flocks now. Glory to God for this wonderful thing!

Shepherd 2   Blessed be God, who is rich in love and mercy!

(Shepherds exit.)

Narrator   Let us always thank God for loving us so much and becoming a human being like us. May we never forget how amazing this is.

Leader's Guide

Background Notes:

The story of the Magi confirms that Jesus is the king, the Messiah who would be born in David's city. Magi was a term for people skilled in supernatural knowledge and power. They weren't kings. The gospel's Magi from the East were probably from Mesopotamia, the home of astrology. A popular belief was that a new star appeared whenever a person was born. When the star appears, the Magi go to the Jewish people to find out about the Messiah. The Jewish prophets tell them that the king is to be born in Bethlehem. Only after the Magi are in Jerusalem does the star guide them to the house where Jesus is.

In Matthew's gospel, it is the Gentiles, not the shepherds, who first worship Jesus. The Magi prostrate themselves before him. The three presents they bring have led to the belief that there were three Magi. Tradition has even named them Caspar, Melchior, and Balthasar. Their gifts are interpreted as symbols of the child. There is gold, for a king, frankincense, for God; and myrrh, a sweet-smelling resin used in anointing for burial, to signify his death.

The conflict between Jesus and official Judaism is already present in the infancy narratives as Herod makes plans to murder the new king of the Jews.

The feast of Epiphany (manifestation of God) is called Little Christmas. It is January 6 or in the United States a Sunday between January 2 and 8. Some people exchange gifts on this day. Priests may give an Epiphany house blessing in which they write a code like 19 + C + M + B + 99 above the door. The letters represent the Magi; the numbers, the year; and the crosses (like compass points), all nations.

Times for Use: Epiphany, lessons on the infancy narratives, the good news, the identity of Jesus, missionary work, Gentiles.

CAST	PROPS
Narrator	Star
Magi 1, 2, 3+	Chair
Herod	Doll or blanket for child
Priests 1, 2+	Three Gifts to represent gold,
Scribes 1, 2+	myrrh, and frankincense
Mary	

QUESTIONS FOR CHILDREN

Before the play: In a Nativity scene we usually see three kings nearby. Who do they represent? What nationality of people did Jesus come to save? What kind of king is Jesus, whom the Magi came to honor?

After the play: What gifts did the Magi give to Jesus? What gifts can you give to God? What in the story of the Epiphany suggests the conflict and suffering that Jesus will face?

CLASS PRAYER

Gathered around a nativity scene, hold a prayer service for missionaries:

• Sing "We Three Kings."
• Pray: God, may people everywhere come to know you. Bless missionaries as they work to spread the Good News of your love. Bless their efforts with success. We pray today especially for missionary work in the countries of (students name countries).
• The students place money for the missions and/or promises of good deeds as a gift in a basket in front of a nativity scene.

The Visit of the Magi

MATTHEW 2:1–12

(Priest 1 and Scribe 1 are on stage.)

| Narrator | After Jesus was born in Bethlehem of Judea, in the days of King Herod, Magi, wise men from the East, came to Jerusalem. |

(Magi enter and go to Priest 1 and Scribe 1.)

Magi 1	Where is the newborn king of the Jews?
Magi 2	We saw his star at its rising and have come to pay him homage.
Priest 1	I don't know anything about him.

(Magi exit.)

| Priest 1 | (to Scribe 1) We'd better tell King Herod about this. |

(Priest 1 and Scribe 1 exit.)

| Narrator | When King Herod was told, he was greatly troubled, and all Jerusalem was, too. |

(King Herod, Priest 1, and Scribe 1 enter.)

| King Herod | Have all the chief priests and the scribes come here. |
| Priest 1 | Yes, your Highness. |

(Priest 1 and Scribe 1 exit. Priests and Scribes enter and stand before King Herod. Messenger enters and stands in back.)

King Herod	Tell me, where is the Messiah to be born?
Priest 2	In Bethlehem of Judea.
Scribe 2	For a prophet wrote, "And you, Bethlehem, land of Judah, are by no means least among the rulers of Judah. From you shall come a ruler who is to shepherd my people Israel."
King Herod	Go. That's all I wanted to know.

(All except Messenger exit.)

19

King Herod   (to Messenger) Come here.

(Messenger goes to King Herod.)

King Herod   Find those Magi from the East and have them come here. Don't let anyone know I sent you.

Messenger   Yes, your Highness. (Exits.)

King Herod   (pacing back and forth) A new king! I must get rid of him.

(Messenger and Magi enter.)

King Herod   (to Magi) Thank you for coming. Naturally I'm interested in the new king. When did you see the star appear?

Narrator   Herod learned about the star from the Magi.

King Herod   Go to Bethlehem and search carefully for the child. When you have found him, bring me word, so that I too may go and pay him homage.

Magi 1   We'll be glad to.

(Magi bow, and King Herod and Messenger exit. Magi walk a little way.)

Magi 3   (excitedly) Look! There's the star again!

Magi 1   It's moving ahead of us.

Magi 2   To guide us to the newborn king.

(Mary enters with child and sits in the background. Magi continue to walk.)

Magi 1   It stopped moving.

Magi 2   It's right above this house. Let's see who lives here.

(Magi go to Mary, "knock" on door.)

Mary   Come in.

(Magi enter and and kneel.)

Magi 3   Hail, king of the Jews!

Magi 2   We bring you gifts from our country.

Magi 1   Gold. (Presents gold.)

Magi 2   Frankincense. (Presents frankincense.)

Magi 3   And myrrh. (Presents myrrh.)

(Mary smiles and accepts the gifts.)

Narrator   The Magi were warned in a dream not to return to Herod, so they went back to their country by another way. When Herod realized that the Magi had tricked him, he was furious. He had all boys two years and under who lived in and around Bethlehem killed. But Mary, Joseph, and Jesus escaped to Egypt. This story of the wise men from the East teaches us that God came to save people of all nations. It is up to us to make God known to them.

Leader's Guide

Background Notes:

Mary and Joseph take Jesus to Jerusalem for his presentation. In this ceremony the firstborn son is consecrated to the Lord. This was in memory of the Passover when the angel of the Lord did not slay the firstborn of the Israelites. Actually, Jesus has always belonged to the Father, but Mary and Joseph fulfill the Jewish Law. They offer not a lamb but the offering of the poor: a pair of turtledoves. Simeon, a devout man who had difficult days of service in the Temple was inspired by the Spirit to come to the Temple, when Jesus was there. The Spirit had revealed to Simeon that he would not die until he had seen the Savior. As all rabbis did when blessing children, Simeon takes Jesus into his arms and blesses God. His canticle declares universal salvation. In blessing the parents, Simeon predicts the child's destiny and foretells that Mary will be linked with Jesus in his redemptive suffering. The church, too, experiences his suffering and sorrow. Simeon, symbol of old Israel, having witnessed the fulfillment of God's promises, can depart in peace.

Anna, a holy widow, recognizes the Messiah and thanks God. From that day she proclaims the good news to all who wait for salvation. Simeon and Anna were members of the anawim, a small group of Israel's faithful people who had kept alive God's promise.

Christians pray Simeon's prayer, the *Nunc Dimittis*, every day in the Night Prayer of the Liturgy of the Hours. We do not need to hope for a savior. We live in the ages after he has appeared. With Simeon we are grateful and happy that God has sent a savior. Simeon's canticle is also a prayer for the dying.

Times for Use: After Christmas, on the Feast of the Presentation (Candlemas Day), lessons on the infancy narratives, Mary, obedience to law, poverty, the identity of Jesus, faithfulness, the suffering of Jesus.

QUESTIONS FOR CHILDREN

Before the play: When was the first time you went to church? Why did you go? What are some rules and customs your family follows because it is Catholic?

After the play: Why did Mary and Joseph take Jesus to the Temple? What are some Catholic customs associated with a baby's becoming a child of God? How were Simeon and Anna rewarded for being faithful to God? What sorrows would Mary have to endure because she was the mother of Jesus?

CLASS PRAYER

Pray Simeon's Canticle. You might pray for the intention that all those who do not yet know Jesus may come to hear and accept the Good News. This would include people in mission countries as well as people in the students' families.

Simeon's Canticle

Master, now you are dismissing your servant in peace,
　according to your word;
for my eyes have seen your salvation,
　which you have prepared in the presence of all people,
a light for revelation to the Gentiles
　and for glory to your people Israel.

CAST	PROPS
Narrator	**Doll or blanket for baby**
baby	**Two birds in a cage**
Mary	
Joseph	
Simeon	
Anna	

The Presentation

LUKE 2:22–38

(Mary and Joseph enter. Joseph carries the birds, and Mary holds the baby.)

Narrator   It was a Jewish law that every boy should be offered to God soon after birth and that a lamb or two birds be sacrificed. Mary and Joseph brought baby Jesus to Jerusalem to present him to the Lord. A holy man named Simeon was waiting for the savior of Israel. The Holy Spirit let him know that he would not die until he had seen the Messiah. On the day that Mary and Joseph came to the Temple, the Spirit led Simeon there.

(Simeon enters, goes to Mary and Joseph, and smiling takes the baby into his arms.)

Simeon   (with great joy)
Blessed be the God of Israel!
Master, now you are dismissing your servant in peace,
according to your word,
for my eyes have seen your salvation,
(raises baby in front of him)
which you prepared in the presence of all peoples,
a light for revelation to the Gentiles,
and for glory to your people Israel.
(Places baby in Mary's arms)

Mary   (surprised) What amazing things to say about my son!

Joseph   (to Mary) Remarkable! I wonder how he knows.

Simeon   (putting his hand on Mary's and Joseph's heads) May God bless you both and make you good parents. (turns to Mary) This child is destined for the falling and rising of many in Israel. He will be a sign that will be opposed, so that the secret thoughts of many people will be revealed. A sword will pierce your heart too.

Narrator   Anna, a prophetess who was eighty-four years old, was in the Temple. She had moved there long ago after her husband died. She never left the Temple but fasted and prayed there night and day.

(Anna enters and goes to Mary and Joseph.)

Anna   (raising arms) Thanks be to our great and good God! May I hold your baby?

(Mary gives Anna the baby.)

Anna   (smiling and rocking the baby) Wait until the others hear. They will be so glad that our redeemer has finally come.

Narrator   Simeon and Anna had been faithful to God. They were rewarded by seeing the Messiah they had longed for. They remind us to stay close to Jesus, to obey God's commands, and to sing God's praises.

Leader's Guide

Background Notes:

Jewish people were obliged to travel to Jerusalem for three major feasts: Passover, Pentecost, and Tabernacles. Passover was celebrated for eight days in honor of the Exodus. Mary, Joseph, and Jesus go to Jerusalem for Passover when Jesus is twelve years old, a year before he officially reaches manhood. This visit foreshadows Jesus' going to Jerusalem for Passover at the end of his life, where he would undergo his own passover from death to life. On the way home, Mary and Joseph discover that Jesus is missing. In a caravan men and women often traveled separately. Probably Mary assumed Jesus was with Joseph and Joseph thought he was with her. They search for him for three days—a time symbolic of the resurrection. Mary and Joseph find Jesus in the Temple, talking to the teachers. He explains to them that he is about his mission: his Father's work. Here he is not referring to his father Joseph, but he is calling God his father for the first time. He claims divine sonship. The gospel says that Mary and Joseph do not understand what Jesus meant. Mary must have thought with sorrow of her future separation from him. She ponders the mystery she is sharing in.

Jesus returns to Nazareth with his parents. There, under their guidance, he grows in all ways to perfect manhood. He is always ready to do the Father's will.

Times for Use: Before the Feast of the Holy Family, lessons on the infancy narratives, the identity of Jesus, obedience, Mary, ministry.

QUESTIONS FOR CHILDREN

Before the play: Did your parents ever lose you or one of your brothers or sisters? How do you think they felt? How did they react when they found their missing child?

After the play: Why did Jesus stay behind in Jerusalem? In what ways do you think Jesus was obedient to Mary and Joseph when they returned to Nazareth? How can you imitate Jesus' obedience?

CLASS PRAYER

Jesus, when you were my age, you obeyed your parents even though you were God. By this you show me how important you consider obedience. When we obey our parents, we are obeying our heavenly Father, whose fourth commandment is "Honor your father and mother." Thank you for my parents. Through their love and care you show your love for me. Help me to return that love by loving my parents. Give me your grace to love them enough to obey them, especially at those times when what my parents tell me to do is hard for me to do or is something I don't understand. This is the mission you give me today as a child in my family.

(You might invite the students to reflect in their hearts on the time it is most difficult for them to obey. Encourage them to resolve to try harder and to trust in the Holy Spirit for help.)

CAST   PROPS

Narrator   **Chairs for Jesus and**
Jesus   **Teachers**
Mary
Joseph
Relative+
Uncle
John
Teachers 1, 2+

The Boy Jesus in the Temple

LUKE 2:41–52

(Jesus is seated on a chair off to the side. Teachers are seated around him.)

Narrator Jewish people went to Jerusalem every year for the feast of Passover. Mary and Joseph went too. When Jesus was twelve, he went with them. On the way home, at the end of the first day of travel, Mary and Joseph missed Jesus.

(Joseph enters. Mary enters a little later.)

Mary (worried) Joseph, isn't Jesus with you?

Joseph (shaking head) No, Mary. I haven't seen him since we left. He's probably with his cousins. Don't worry. He must be somewhere in this caravan.

Mary Let's look for him.

(Relative 1 enters.)

Mary (to Relative 1) Have you seen Jesus?

Relative 1 (shaking head) No, not all day. (Exits)

(Uncle enters)

Joseph (to Uncle) We're looking for our son. Has he been with you?

Uncle No, sorry. I haven't seen him. Let me ask John. (Calls) John, come here a minute.

(John enters running and goes to Uncle.)

Uncle (to John) Son, Joseph here is looking for Jesus. Was he playing with you and the others today?

John No, Dad. He wasn't with us.

Mary (wringing hands) Joseph, I'm frightened. We better go back to Jerusalem to look for him.

(Uncle and John exit. Mary and Joseph walk around.)

Narrator Mary and Joseph searched for Jesus all over Jerusalem for three days. Finally they found him in the Temple sitting in the midst of the teachers.

26

Teacher 1	(to Jesus) Yahweh is a mighty God.
Teacher 2	Yes. We must follow his commands carefully.
Jesus	True, but is it better to serve out of fear (puts out hand) or out of love (puts out other hand)?
Teacher 1	(to Teacher 2) How can one so young be so wise?
	(Mary sees Jesus.)
Mary	(pointing to Jesus) Look over there. He's with the teachers. It seems as if he is teaching them.
Joseph	I don't know what to say!
	(Mary and Joseph walk quickly to Jesus.)
Mary	(shaking finger at Jesus) Child, why have you treated us like this? Your father and I have been looking for you, worried to death.
Jesus	(surprised) Why? Did you not know that I must be in my Father's house?
	(Mary and Joseph look at each other.)
Joseph	(to Mary) What does that mean?
Mary	(shrugs shoulders) I don't know.
Joseph	(taking Jesus by the arm) It's time we went home, Son. Let's go.
Narrator	Jesus went with Mary and Joseph to Nazareth and was obedient to them. Mary kept all these things in her heart. And Jesus grew in wisdom and age and favor before God and people. Let us pray for the grace to obey like Jesus, to listen to God and the people God has set in authority over us.

The Public Life
of Jesus

Leader's Guide

Background Notes:

John carries on the role of Isaiah and Elijah. The greatest prophet, he prepares people for the Messiah. He preaches conversion and repentance, a complete internal turning of the heart toward God. His baptism is a sign of this repentance. John claims that the one to come is mightier than he in the war against evil. John is not worthy even to be his slave and untie his sandals. When Jesus asks for baptism, John recognizes him.

Although Jesus, being sinless, has no need of repentance, and therefore no need of baptism, he acts as humanity's representative. He identifies himself with sinners. His baptism is an acceptance of the human condition. Going down into the water symbolized the death humanity deserved. At the baptism of Jesus, the Holy Spirit, who overshadowed Mary at his conception, overshadows him to begin his mission. On Pentecost the Spirit will come to the church and anoint the followers of Jesus for mission. Jesus' baptism is an acceptance of his mission as Messiah.

Jesus goes down into the water. When he comes up, God declares him "my beloved Son." In Christian baptism we, too, are claimed as sons and daughters of God. But, unlike John's baptism, our baptism actually gives us the gift of the Spirit.

Eastern Churches celebrate the mystery of Christ's baptism on the Epiphany. Epiphany means "manifestation." In the synoptic gospels, the Trinity is manifested at Jesus' baptism. The Father (the voice), the Son (Jesus), and the Holy Spirit (the dove) are all present. The Trinity has been named in the formula for Christian baptism since apostolic times: "I baptize you in the name of the Father, and of the Son, and of the Holy Spirit."

Times for Use: Lessons on the identity of Jesus, John the Baptist, humility, conversion, mission of Jesus, baptism, the Holy Spirit.

CAST   PROPS

Narrator   **Large seashell**
John
Jesus
Priest
Person
Crowd+
Voice

QUESTIONS FOR CHILDREN

Before the play: What stories do you know about your baptism—where it took place, who was there, whether you cried? What was your baptism a sign of?

After the play: What did Jesus' baptism signify? How was John's baptism different from the baptism you received? How can you tell whether someone is really repentant and converted? What might John the Baptist say to us today?

CLASS PRAYER

Hold a baptismal ritual.

•Play a song about the new life of baptism and/or being a follower of Jesus, such as "New Life," "In Him We Live," "I Say Yes, Lord," "Here I Am, Lord," "I Have Decided to Follow Jesus"

•Invite the students to renew their baptismal vows and profession of faith by answering "I do" to the following questions:

> Do you reject Satan?
> And all his works?
> And all his empty promises?
> Do you believe in God the Father almighty, creator of heaven and earth?
> Do you believe in Jesus Christ, his only Son, our Lord, who was born of the Virgin Mary, was crucified, died, and was buried, rose from the dead, and is now seated at the right hand of the Father?
> Do you believe in the Holy Spirit, the holy Catholic Church, the communion of saints, the forgiveness of sins, the resurrection of the body, and life everlasting?

•Bless the students with holy water as a reminder of their baptism and their mission to be Christians.

The Baptism of Jesus

MATTHEW 3:4–17 MARK 1:4–11 LUKE 3:7–22 JOHN 1:19–34

(John is facing Crowd that includes Person and Priest.)

Narrator	John the Baptist preached in the desert of Judea. He wore clothing made of camel's hair and a leather belt around his waist. He ate locusts and wild honey. The people in the region were being baptized by John in the Jordan River as they admitted their sins.
John	Repent, for the kingdom of heaven is near. Every tree that does not bear good fruit will be cut down (makes chopping motion) and thrown (makes tossing motion) into the fire.
Person 1	What should we do?
John	Whoever has two cloaks (holds up two fingers) should share with the person who has none. And whoever has food should also share.
Priest	Who are you?
John	I am not the Messiah. I am the voice of one crying out in the desert, (cups hand next to mouth) "Make straight the way of the Lord."
Person 1	I am a sinner. But I am sorry. Please baptize me.
	(Person "wades" to John, who "pours water" on Person with seashell.)
John	(to Crowd) I baptize with water as a sign of repentance, but one who is more powerful than I is coming. I am not worthy to undo his sandal strap. (points down) He will baptize you with the Holy Spirit and fire. (raises arms)
Narrator	One day Jesus came from Galilee to John at the Jordan River to be baptized.
	(Jesus enters and goes to John.)
John	(surprised) I need to be baptized by you. How is it that you are coming to me?
Jesus	Let it be so now, for it fulfills the plan.
	(Jesus "wades" into the water toward John, who "pours water" on him.)
Narrator	Suddenly the heavens were opened, and the Spirit of God came down like a dove upon him.

Voice   (loud and low) This is my beloved Son with whom I am well pleased.

(All look up in awe.)

Narrator   With his baptism, Jesus accepted his mission and was filled with power to begin it. At our baptism we received the mission to continue Jesus' work. May we teach others about God and show them God's love.

Leader's Guide

Background Notes:
The temptation story shows the humanity of Jesus. It also depicts Christ's overthrow of Satan's empire. Jesus goes to the desert, the place where evil spirits dwell according to tradition. He is there for forty days, which parallels the forty-year sojourn of the Israelites in the desert. The temptations are given in different orders in Matthew and Luke, but the scriptural answers to each are the same. The temptations test Jesus as Messiah. He is tempted to be a messiah of pleasure (turning stones to bread), a messiah of power (owning nations), and a messiah of fantastic feats (surviving a leap from the Temple parapet). Victoriously, Jesus rejects these temptations and embraces the role of true Messiah, the suffering servant. One day when Peter tries to dissuade him from the path of the cross, Jesus will call Peter Satan.

The outcome of the battle in the desert is demonstrated later in the exorcisms Jesus performs. As members of the church face temptations, they look to Christ's example as he deals with temptations against his mission.

Times for Use: Lent, lessons on temptation, the identity of Jesus, the mission of Jesus.

CAST   PROPS

CAST	PROPS
Narrator	Rocks
Jesus	Two chairs for
Devil	Temple and mountain
Angels 1, 2+	

QUESTIONS FOR CHILDREN

Before the play: Who is Satan? Why is he against us? What is it like to be tempted?

After the play: What were Jesus' temptations? How did he overcome them? What temptations are the greatest for people today, for students today? What helps do we have to resist temptation?

CLASS PRAYER

Pray the following litany with the students. They might add their own prayers. The response is "Lord, lead us not into temptation."

When there are things we'd rather do than go to Sunday Mass…

When we see items in the store that we want but don't have the money to buy…

When someone is making us angry…

When telling the truth might get us or a friend into trouble…

When our younger brother or sister is driving us crazy…

When we have a chance to get even with someone…

When our parents won't let us do what others our age do…

When there is a movie or a magazine or a book that we know we shouldn't see…

When it is easy for us to cheat…

Let us pray. Lord, you did not give into temptation. When we are tempted to do wrong, make us strong like you. More than anything we want to be good Christians and live with you forever. Sometimes, though, it is hard for us to do what is right. We are weak. We need the power of your grace to help us resist temptation. By your cross you conquered evil forever. Never let it conquer us.

The Temptation of Jesus

(Jesus kneels, praying)

Narrator After his baptism, Jesus was led by the Spirit into the desert for forty days. He ate nothing during those days and was very hungry.

(Devil enters and goes to Jesus. Jesus looks surprised.)

Devil (picking up rock) If you are the Son of God, command these stones to become loaves of bread.

Jesus (in a strong voice) It is written, "One does not live by bread alone, but by every word that comes from the mouth of God."

Devil Come with me.

Narrator The devil then took Jesus to the Temple in the holy city and had him stand on the edge of the roof.

(Jesus and Devil stand on chairs.)

Devil If you are the Son of God, throw yourself down from here. For it is written, "He will command his angels to guard you," and "With their hands they will support you so that you will not dash your foot against a stone."

Jesus (with a strong voice) Again it is written, "You shall not put the Lord, your God, to the test."

(Devil shrugs and shakes head. The Devil and Jesus step off chairs and walk around.)

Narrator Then the devil took Jesus to a very high mountain.

(Jesus and Devil stand on chairs again.)

Devil (making a wide sweeping motion outward) Look at all these kingdoms of the world and their splendor. All these I will give you, if you will fall down and worship me.

Jesus (shouting and pointing) Get away, Satan! It is written, "Worship the Lord your God, and serve only him."

(Devil stomps out angrily.)

Narrator Angels came and waited on Jesus. When we are tempted, Jesus knows what we are going through. We can always turn to him for help.

(Angels enter and bow before Jesus.)

Leader's Guide

Background Notes:
The first disciples of Jesus originally were John's disciples. They accept Jesus and call him Rabbi, the title of a teacher. Andrew and the other disciple (perhaps John) respond to Christ's invitation "Come and see." So memorable is this event that even the hour is included in the gospel. The two disciples probably spend the night with Jesus. The next day, Andrew brings his brother Simon to meet Jesus. Jesus changes Simon's name to Cephas. This name change signifies that Simon is assuming a new way of life.

Nathanael is commonly identified with Bartholomew. When Jesus refers to some personal incident in Nathanael's life ("I saw you under the fig tree"), Nathanael acknowledges him as Son of God and King of Israel. The angels ascending and descending on the Son of Man is a reference to Jacob's ladder. In a vision, the patriarch Jacob saw a ladder, a mediator between God and human beings. The "far greater things" that Nathanael will see is the glory of God manifested in Jesus, our divine mediator connecting heaven and earth.

Times for Use: Lessons on discipleship, the apostles, the identity of Jesus, Peter, vocations.

CAST / PROPS

CAST	PROPS
Narrator	Table
Jesus	Three chairs
John	Tree or drawing of tree
Disciple	on board
Andrew	
Simon Peter	
Philip	
Nathanael	

QUESTIONS FOR CHILDREN

Before the play: How did you come to know about Jesus? Why do you think people were attracted to Jesus? Who were some of his closest followers? How did they show strengths and weaknesses?

After the play: What does it mean to be a follower of Jesus? Why have you chosen to follow Jesus? Have you brought anyone else to meet him? How could you introduce others to Jesus?

CLASS PRAYER

Read the following adaptation of "One Solitary Life" and have the students reflect on Jesus.

He was born in a small village. He worked in a carpenter shop until he was thirty. He then became a traveling preacher. He never held an office. He never had a family or owned a house. He didn't go to college. He had no credentials but himself.

He was only thirty-three when the public turned against him. His friends ran away. He was turned over to his enemies and went through the mockery of a trial. He was nailed to a cross between two thieves. While he was dying, his executioners gambled for his clothing, the only property he had on earth. He was laid in a borrowed grave.

Twenty centuries have come and gone, and today he is the central figure of the human race. All the armies that ever marched, all the navies that ever sailed, all the parliaments that ever sat, and all the kings that ever reigned have not affected life on earth as much as that one solitary life.

—Source unknown

The First Apostles

JOHN 1:35–51

(John, Andrew, and Disciple are standing talking together.)

Narrator   One day John was with two of his disciples.

(Jesus enters and walks by. John stops talking and watches Jesus pass.)

John   (gesturing toward Jesus) Look, here is the Lamb of God.

(Andrew and Disciple wave to John and run after Jesus. They follow him a while. John exits.)

Jesus   (turning) What are you looking for?

(Andrew and Disciple look at each other.)

Andrew   Rabbi…

Disciple   Teacher, where are you staying?

Jesus   (laughing) Come and see.

(Jesus, Andrew, and Disciple walk on for a while, then sit at the table.)

Narrator   They stayed with Jesus that day. It was about 4:00 in the afternoon.

(Andrew and Disciple rise, wave, and leave. Jesus stands. Simon Peter enters. Andrew runs to him. Jesus sits.)

Andrew   Here you are. We have found the Messiah. Come on. You have to meet him.

(Andrew grabs Simon Peter by the arm and they walk to Jesus. Jesus rises.)

Andrew   Jesus, this is my brother Simon.

(Jesus and Simon shake hands.)

Jesus   (looking into Simon's eyes) You are Simon, son of John. You are to be called Peter.

(All exit.)

Narrator   The next day Jesus decided to go to Galilee. He found Philip who lived in Bethsaida where Andrew and Peter lived.

(Jesus enters from one side and Philip from another. Nathanael enters and stands at a distance under the tree.)

Jesus   (to Philip as they pass each other) Follow me.

(Philip turns around and walks with Jesus for a while.)

Philip   I'll see you later.

(Philip leaves Jesus and goes to Nathanael. Jesus sits.)

Philip   (to Nathanael) We have found the one about whom Moses in the law and also the prophets wrote. He is Jesus, son of Joseph, from Nazareth.

Nathanael   Can anything good come from Nazareth?

Philip   Come and see.

(Philip and Nathanael approach Jesus.)

Jesus   Here is a true Israelite. There is no falseness in him.

Nathanael   How do you know me?

Jesus   (rising) Before Philip called you, I saw you under the fig tree.

Nathanael   (excitedly) Rabbi, you are the Son of God! You are the King of Israel!

Jesus   Do you believe because I told you that I saw you under the fig tree? You will see greater things than this. Amen, amen, I tell you, you will see the sky opened (raises hand) and the angels of God ascending and descending upon the Son of Man.

Narrator   We, too, are disciples of Jesus. May we learn to know and love him more each day and lead others to him.

(All exit, Jesus' arm around Nathanael's shoulder.)

Leader's Guide

Background Notes:

The three disciples who form the inner circle (Peter, James, and John) appear in this account of the call of the first disciples. Two sets of brothers are involved: Peter and Andrew as well as James and John. As Jesus passes by, he calls these men to follow him. His call and their response are direct and immediate. The fishermen drop everything to come after Jesus. They probably already knew him. Jesus' power over them motivates them to leave their jobs and their homes to follow him. Discipleship can demand renunciation of possessions and family ties. Jesus promises to make these disciples fishers of people, a hint of their apostolic authority and missionary work.

Ordinarily disciples choose their master. Here Jesus reverses the situation and chooses his disciples. He chooses not learned rabbis but blue-collar workers. Fishing was a major industry in Galilee. The four fishermen in this story own their own nets and have employees. They are apparently successful at their trade but are willing to sacrifice all in order to commit themselves to Jesus. Their nets do not hold them captive.

Times for Use: Lessons on discipleship, ministry, the apostles, vocations.

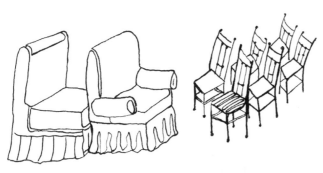

CAST

Narrator
Jesus
Peter
Andrew
James
John
Zebedee
Hired Men 1, 2+

PROPS

Rows of chairs representing two boats

nets

QUESTIONS FOR CHILDREN

Before the play: What might you have to give up to follow Jesus? Would this be hard to do? Why would you do it? Did you ever think of becoming a priest, a deacon, or a religious sister or brother? How do these people serve Jesus?

After the play: What did the apostles give up to follow Jesus? What role did they play in the church? How does Jesus call people today? How can you be a fisher of people for Jesus?

CLASS PRAYER

Have the students sing or listen to "Lord, You Have Come (*Pescador De Hombres*)" or another song about following Christ. Then invite them to respond, "Jesus, I will follow you" to the following words of Jesus in the Gospels:

Repent, for the kingdom of heaven has come near. (Matthew 4:17)…

Those who eat my flesh and drink my blood have eternal life. (John 6:54)…

Strive first for the kingdom of God and his righteousness. (Matthew 6:33)…

Let your light shine before others. (Matthew 5:16)…

Do not store up for yourselves treasures on earth… but treasures in heaven. (Matthew 6:19–20)…

Love one another. (John 13:34)…

Do not judge. (Matthew 7:1)…

Ask, and it will be given you. (Matthew 7:7)…

Do to others as you would have them do to you. (Matthew 7:12)…

Go, sell your possessions, and give the money to the poor. (Matthew 19:21)…

You ought to wash one another's feet. (John 13:14)…

Forgive, if you have anything against anyone. (Mark 11:25)…

Love your enemies and pray for those who persecute you. (Matthew 5:44)…

Follow me. (Matthew 4:19)…

The Call of the First Apostles

MATTHEW 4:18–22 MARK 1:16–20

(Peter and Andrew are in one boat. James, John, Zebedee, and Hired Men 1, 2 are mending nets in the other boat some distance away.)

Narrator   The brothers Peter and Andrew were fishing one day on the Sea of Galilee. They were fishermen. The brothers James and John were with their father, Zebedee, and some hired man mending their nets.

(Jesus enters. Peter and Andrew cast a net into the sea while Jesus watches.)

Jesus   (calling to Peter and Andrew) Follow me, and I will make you fishers of people.

(Jesus walks on. Peter and Andrew climb out of boat and catch up to Jesus. They all walk over to the other boat.)

Jesus   (shouting) James! John! Come follow me, and I will make you fishers of people.

James   (to Zebedee) Dad, we must go.

Zebedee   God be with you, boys!

(James and John get out of boat, wave to Zebedee, and follow Jesus. Zebedee waves back.)

Narrator   All the fishermen Jesus called immediately went off in his company, leaving their jobs and their homes. They became his apostles, the twelve men Jesus chose to lead his church. May we always show great love and respect for our church leaders and follow their guidance.

Leader's Guide

Background Notes:
In the gospels of Luke and Mark, Matthew is called Levi. When Jesus calls Matthew to follow him, Matthew leaves his tax collector's booth as promptly as the fishermen left their nets. As a tax collector, Matthew was considered a traitor, a social outcast, and a sinner. He collected taxes from his own people for the oppressor Rome. His profit was made by extorting more than what was legally due. By choosing Matthew to follow him and by accepting his dinner invitation, Jesus underlines the fact that he came for sinners. The upright Jewish person did not associate or eat with sinners and Gentiles. But Jesus calls everyone to the messianic banquet. In particular he goes out to the marginalized people, those whom others ignore and prefer to forget. We all must admit we are sinners before we can go to Jesus.

Matthew's wholehearted commitment to Christ involves a conversion. He reorients his life. He chooses to forsake the wicked ways of the tax booth and become a doer of good. In fact, Matthew becomes a leader in calling other sinners to hear the good news and change their hearts.

Times for Use: Lessons on discipleship, conversion, the mission of Jesus, vocations.

QUESTIONS FOR CHILDREN

Before the play: Who are some people whom others avoided and Jesus went out to? Why didn't the Jewish people like tax collectors?

After the play: Why do you think Matthew responded so promptly to Jesus?
How should we regard sinners? How should we treat them?

CLASS PRAYER

Jesus, following you has a price. You call us away from our sinful situations. We all have our tax booths. Maybe we are chained to stealing, cheating, lying, or disobeying. Maybe we are far apart from God and seldom pray or celebrate the Eucharist. Maybe we are hurting ourselves by other bad habits. Maybe we are proud, stubborn, or selfish. Give us the grace to change. Make us truly alive by leaving those things that make us less than we could be. Let us live a good Christian life, walking in your footsteps, bringing life and love to others.

(Invite the students to speak to Jesus in their hearts about one thing in their lives they need to change to be a better disciple of his.)

CAST	PROPS
Narrator	**Two or more tables**
Jesus	**Chairs**
Matthew	
Sinners 1, 2+	
Disciples 1, 2+	
Pharisees 1, 2+	

The Call of Matthew

MATTHEW 9:9–13 MARK 2:14-17 LUKE 5:27–32

(Matthew sits behind table.)

Narrator Matthew was a tax collector. Jewish people did not like Jewish men who collected taxes for their conqueror, Rome. Often these tax collectors kept some money for themselves. One day Matthew was sitting at the tax booth.

(Jesus and Disciples enter. Jesus goes to Matthew.)

Jesus (to Matthew) Follow me.

(Matthew stands and follows Jesus.)

Matthew (to Jesus) Master, please come to my house for dinner.

(All walk to other table and sit. Sinners enter and sit with Jesus and Disciples. Pharisees enter and sit apart.)

Narrator While Jesus was at table in Matthew's house, many tax collectors and sinners came and sat with Jesus and his disciples.

(Pharisees 1, 2 stand and go to Disciples.)

Pharisee 1 (to Disciple 1) Why does your teacher eat with tax collectors and sinners?

(Jesus looks up at Pharisees.)

Jesus (to Pharisees) Those who are well do not need a physician, but those are sick do. Go and learn the meaning of the words "I desire mercy, not sacrifice." I have not come to call the righteous, but sinners.

(Pharisees return to places, shaking heads.)

Narrator Jesus shows us that it is good to reach out to people who are not accepted by others. They may become our good friends.

Leader's Guide

REJECTION AT NAZARETH

Background Notes:

The Jewish people met in local synagogues for prayer. The sabbath synagogue service in the first century seems to have included a reading from the Torah, a reading from the prophets, and a sermon on the meaning of the readings. Rows of people sat around the perimeter of the room, leaving the center empty for the speakers. Jesus acts as teacher by doing the reading and explaining it in such a way that people marvel at his wisdom. The people are amazed that this man, Mary's son, who grew up among them could offer them words of salvation.

In Luke the passage Jesus reads is a combination of Isaiah 61:1–2 and 58:6. These verses reflect the jubilee year which is celebrated every fifty years. During this year fields lay fallow, persons returned home, debts were canceled, and slaves set free. In Jesus God has fulfilled his promise. His townspeople, however, lack faith in him.

Jesus explains that the prophets Elijah and Elisha ministered to non-Jewish people. Just as prophets were rejected in the Old Testament times, so too is Jesus rejected. The people are offended and enraged when he implies that salvation is not for them alone. Foreigners too would be welcomed into God's kingdom. The opposition Jesus experiences in Nazareth foreshadows the rest of his life. But just as he escapes from death at the hands of his neighbors, in the end he is victorious over death by his resurrection.

Times for Use: Lessons on the mission of Jesus, the suffering of Jesus.

CAST

PROPS

Narrator
Jesus
Persons
1, 2, 3+

At least two rows of chairs

QUESTIONS FOR CHILDREN

Before the play: What did Jesus come to teach us? Who are some people who rejected him? Why do you think they did this? How do we reject him today?

After the play: How do the phrases in Isaiah apply to Jesus? What would a mission statement for ourselves include?

CLASS PRAYER

Read the following reflection and prayer slowly with pauses.

The mission of Jesus is my mission.
The Spirit of the Lord is upon me, because he anoints me
in the sacraments of Baptism and Confirmation.
I am anointed to bring good news to the poor,
to show all kinds of needy people by my love for them
that they are rich in God's love.
God has sent me to proclaim release to the captives,
to tell people who are imprisoned
in mental or physical pain and suffering
that God has conquered sin and death.
God has sent me to give sight to the blind,
to get people to see the truths
that there is a loving God,
that they are saved,
and that they are to live as Christ taught.
God has sent me to let the oppressed go free,
to work to help those who are scorned and taken advantage of.
God has sent me to proclaim the year of the Lord's favor,
to show by my faith, love, and joy
that God has redeemed us and we will live forever.

Jesus, bless my efforts to carry on your work. Make the people whose lives I touch open to the good news I bring by my words and deeds.

Rejection at Nazareth

(Jesus and Persons are seated in two or more rows facing one another across a space.)

Narrator   Jesus had been teaching successfully in synagogues in Galilee. Then he returned to Nazareth, his hometown. On the sabbath he went as usual to the synagogue. There he was handed the scroll of the prophet Isaiah to read.

(Jesus stands and moves to the center area. Person 1 hands him a scroll. Jesus opens the scroll horizontally.)

Jesus   The Spirit of the Lord is upon me,
because he has anointed me
to bring good news to the poor.
He has sent me to proclaim release to the captives
and recovery of sight to the blind,
to let the oppressed go free,
to proclaim the year of the Lord's favor.

(Rolls up the scroll, hands it to Person 1, and sits. All look at Jesus.)

Today this Scripture has been fulfilled in your hearing.

Person 2   Jesus is such a wonderful teacher. Where did he get all this knowledge?

Person 3   Isn't this Joseph's son?

Jesus   You will probably quote to me this proverb, "Doctor, cure yourself!" And you will say, "Do here also in your hometown the things that we have heard you did in Capernaum."

Truly I tell you, no prophet is accepted in the prophet's hometown. When there was a famine in Israel there were many widows, but Elijah was sent only to the widow in Sidon. There were many lepers in the time of Elisha the prophet, but none of them was cleaned except Naaman the Syrian.

(Persons look at one another with eyebrows raised. They frown.)

Person 2   (angrily) How dare he speak this way to us!

Person 3   (pointing) Jesus, get out of our synagogue!

Person 2   (shaking fist) Get out of our town!

Persons   (standing and shaking fists) Get out! Get out!

                   (Persons gather around Jesus and move him off stage.)

Narrator   The people drove Jesus out of the town to the brow of the hill. They intended to hurl him off the cliff. But Jesus passed through their midst and went on his way. May we have the courage to speak the truth even when others do not accept it.

Leader's Guide

Background Notes:

Nicodemus is a leader of the Jews, probably a member of the Sanhedrin, the Jewish council. His calling Jesus "rabbi" shows he accepts Jesus as a teacher. Nicodemus believes that Jesus works miracles because God was with him. Because Jewish officials opposed Jesus, Nicodemus goes to him for in search of truth under cover of the night.

Jesus explains faith to Nicodemus. The word for spirit in Hebrew and in Greek also means wind. Through the Spirit we are born from above. Only if we are born from above can we have eternal life in the kingdom of God. We must become like children again. Faith calls for a spiritual rebirth, not a physical rebirth.

Jesus refers to his sacrifice on the cross. He is the light that dispels the darkness of sin and death.

Later Nicodemus appears in the gospels as someone who has seen the light. The chief priest and Pharisees try to arrest Jesus while he is speaking in the Temple area during the Feast of Tabernacles. Nicodemus speaks out on his behalf, pointing out that Jesus should have a fair hearing before being condemned. Then, after the crucifixion, Nicodemus brings myrrh and aloes to anoint the body of Jesus.

Times for Use: Lessons on the mission of Jesus, faith, the Holy Spirit, baptism.

CAST   PROPS

Narrator   **Two chairs**
Jesus
Nicodemus

QUESTIONS FOR CHILDREN

Before the play: How is Jesus light for us? If you had a private meeting with Jesus, what questions might you have for him? How can you speak to Jesus today and grow in faith?

After the play: How does faith sometimes demand taking risks? When does the Holy Spirit work in us? How?

CLASS PRAYER

Lead the students in the following imaginative prayer:

Close your eyes if you wish and imagine that like Nicodemus you are going in the dark of night to the house where Jesus is. You are in search of some truths about life. There are some things you just don't understand. The stars are out, and it is a pleasant evening. You walk down a narrow deserted street and come to a small, stone house. The door is open as though Jesus is waiting for you. Light is pouring out from it. Jesus is standing in the doorway. When he sees you, he smiles. He welcomes you in and has you sit down. He sits beside you. Looking at his kind, concerned face, you know you can talk to him about anything. Speak to Jesus now in your heart. You might ask him questions. You might talk about anything that is bothering you. You might ask his help, thank him, tell him you love him. [Pause.]

Nicodemus

(Jesus is seated on one of two chairs.)

Narrator   The Pharisee Nicodemus was a leader of the Jewish people. One night he came to visit Jesus.

(Nicodemus enters, looking over his shoulder.)

Jesus   (stands) Nicodemus! Welcome! (gestures to chair) Please, have a seat.

(Nicodemus and Jesus sit.)

Nicodemus   Rabbi, we know that you are a teacher who has come from God. For no one can do the signs that you do if he were apart from God.

Jesus   Very truly, I tell you, no one can see the kingdom of God without being born from above.

Nicodemus   How can anyone be born after he or she is old? Can one enter a second time into the mother and be born again?

Jesus   Very truly, I tell you, no one can enter the kingdom of God without being born of water and Spirit. What is born of the flesh is flesh (hits chest) and what is born of the Spirit is spirit. (points up) Do not be astonished that I said, "You must be born from above." The wind blows where it chooses, and you hear it but you do not know where it comes from or where it goes. So it is with everyone born of the Spirit.

Nicodemus   How can these things be?

Jesus   (shaking head) Are you a teacher of Israel, and yet you do not understand? We speak of what we know and testify to what we have seen, yet you people do not accept our testimony. No one has ascended into heaven except the one who descended from heaven, the Son of Man. (points to self) And just as Moses lifted up the serpent in the wilderness, so must the Son of Man be lifted up, (raises hand) that whoever believes in him may have eternal life.

Nicodemus   (nodding) Ah, yes. Through Moses' serpent of bronze, God healed the people bitten by snakes. You say God will give us eternal life?

Jesus   God so loved the world that he gave his only Son, so that everyone who believes in him may not perish but may have eternal life. Indeed, God did not send the Son into the world to condemn the world, but to save it. Those who do not believe are condemned already. The light has come into the world, but people loved darkness because their deeds were evil. All who do evil hate the light (puts up hand as to ward off light) and do not come to the light, so that their deeds may not be exposed. But those who do good come to the light (raises other hand facing up) so that it may be seen that their deeds were done in God.

Nicodemus   I see you are a wise teacher. I'd like to know more.

(Jesus and Nicodemus stand.)

Jesus   Come back anytime.

(Nicodemus leaves.)

Narrator   Like Nicodemus may we seek to learn more about God by praying, reading the Bible, and studying our faith.

Leader's Guide

Background Notes:

The children the parents bring to Jesus for his blessing could have been infants or boys and girls less than twelve. When the disciples scold the parents, Jesus rebukes his disciples for turning the parents away. Then he embraces the children and blesses them.

No other ancient religious or philosophical teachers have made a point of receiving children this way. Writers in the time of Jesus present children as examples of unreasonable behavior or objects to be trained. Jesus, however, regards them as persons who can enter into a relationship with him and enter the kingdom of God. This particular story is the basis for infant baptism and early first communion.

Children are the little ones of society who had no rights or status in the ancient world. Jesus uses them as the model for his disciples, who had at least once argued about who was the greatest. His followers are to be simple and small, not self-important and power-hungry. They are to be dependent on the Father and open to accepting the gift of the kingdom. In Luke 10:21 Jesus observes that the Father reveals the mysteries of the kingdom not to the learned and wise but to the childlike.

Times for Use: Lessons on holiness, the kingdom, the poor.

QUESTIONS FOR CHILDREN

Before the play: What are some words that describe children? Why do you think children were not afraid to come to Jesus?

After the play: What does this story tell us about Jesus? What must we be like if we wish to enter the kingdom of God? How can we treat children as Jesus did?

CLASS PRAYER

Help the students formulate a litany in which they ask for a childlike heart. Their prayer may take the form, "That we may be _____, we pray, O Lord." Some positive characteristics of a child that the students might name are joyful, open, receptive, spontaneous, dependent, sinless, trusting, loving, full of wonder, simple, and eager to learn.

CAST	PROPS
Narrator	**Doll or blanket for baby**
Jesus	**Two birds in a cage**
Disciples 1, 2+	
Mothers 1, 2, 3+	
Jacob	
Child 1	
Child 2	
Children+	

The Blessing of the Children

MATTHEW 19:13–15 MARK 10:13–16 LUKE 18:15–17

(Jesus and Disciples are seated. Mothers enter holding Children by the hand and carrying babies. Mothers walk to Jesus. Children run.)

Child 1   (pulling Jesus' hand) Come, play with us, Jesus.

Mother 1   (hands on shoulders of Child 2) Master, won't you bless my child?

Mother 2   (holding out baby) Jesus, touch my baby.

Mother 3   (holding Jacob by the hand) Please pray over my son Jacob.

(Disciples stand and gesture to Mothers and Children to go away.)

Disciple 1   (to Mothers) Leave him alone.

Disciple 2   Can't you see how tired he is?

(Mothers and Children start to move away.)

Jesus   (beckoning to Children) Come, children. (to Disciples, sternly) Let the children come to me. Do not stop them, for the kingdom of God belongs to such as these. (gestures to Children) Truly, I tell you, whoever does not accept the kingdom of God as a child will never enter it.

(Jesus takes a baby in his arms. He puts his hand on Child 1's head. Children surround him. Mothers smile at Disciples.)

Narrator   Jesus wants us near him as much as he wanted the children to come to him. Let us never be afraid to go to him and stay close to him.

Leader's Guide

Background Notes:

This event happened at Passover when there were great crowds in Jerusalem. Animals needed for sacrifice were sold in the Court of Gentiles at the Temple: oxen, sheep, and doves. Moneychangers were there because Greek and Roman coins, which bore images, could not be used at the Temple. The whip Jesus used to clear the Temple was probably a symbol of authority, rather than for practical use. In John's gospel, Jesus attacks the institutions, whereas in Mark, he attacks the dishonesty of the dealers. The event shows his zeal as a reformer. In Matthew's gospel, Jesus stays in the Temple healing the blind and the lame after the cleansing.

Jesus refers to God here as "my Father." He calls the Temple a house of prayer. It is not meant to be a market. He says that the Temple is for all nations, an indication of the universality of God's love and salvation. His cleansing is a symbolic action. It implies that the Temple cult no longer has meaning. Prayer and faith are what matter. The temple that Jesus predicts will be raised up after three days is himself. He is the new temple that replaces the Temple. God is found in him.

Times for Use: Lessons on prayer, the church building, the resurrection, the identity of Jesus.

CAST / PROPS

CAST	PROPS
Narrator	Twine for cords
Jesus	Bag of coins
Disciples 1, 2+	Bird cages
Money-changers 1, 2+	Tables
Sellers of doves 1, 2+	Chairs
Jewish persons 1, 2+	
Oxen and sheep	

QUESTIONS FOR CHILDREN

Before the play: What do we do in church to show reverence? How do we behave there?

After the play: Why did Jesus drive the people out of the Temple? Why wasn't Jesus' anger sinful? When should we speak out against what is wrong? Can you give some examples of Christians who have done this?

CLASS PRAYER

Explain that on the way to the Temple for feasts, the people sang hymns. Invite the students to pray the following pilgrim song with you:

How lovely is your dwelling place,
  O LORD of hosts!
My soul longs, indeed it faints
  for the courts of the LORD;
my heart and my flesh sing for joy
  to the living God.

Even the sparrow finds a home,
  and the swallow a nest for herself,
  where she may lay her young,
at your altars, O LORD of hosts,
  my King and my God.
Happy are those who live in your house,
  ever singing your praise.

For a day in your courts is better
  than a thousand elsewhere.
I would rather be a doorkeeper in the house of my God
  than live in the tents of wickedness.
For the LORD God is a sun and shield;
  he bestows favor and honor.
No good thing does the LORD withhold
  from those who walk uprightly.
O LORD of hosts,
  happy is everyone who trusts in you.

Psalm 84:1–5, 10–12

The Cleansing of the Temple

MARK 11:15–18 MATTHEW 21:12–13 LUKE 19:45–46 JOHN 2:13–22

(Money-changers are seated. Sellers of Doves stand behind tables. Bags of coins and cord are on a table. Jesus and Disciples 1, 2 enter and slowly walk toward tables.)

Narrator   Because the feast of Passover was near, Jesus went to Jerusalem. In the temple area he found those who sold oxen, sheep, and doves. Money-changers were also seated there.

(Jesus picks up a cord and waves it in the air.)

Jesus   Out! Get out of here. (Hits table with cord. Pushes table over so coins spill.)

(Money-changers, oxen, and sheep exit in fear.)

Jesus   (angrily to Sellers of Doves) Take these things out of here. Stop making my Father's house a marketplace! It is written, "My house shall be called a house of prayer, but you have made it a den of robbers."

(Sellers of Doves exit.)

Disciple 1   (to Disciple 2) Remember, Scripture says, "Zeal for your house will consume me."

(Jewish Persons 1, 2 enter and go to Jesus.)

Jewish Person 1   What sign can you show us for doing this?

Jesus   Destroy this temple and in three days (holds up three fingers) I will raise it up.

Jewish Person 2   This Temple has been under construction for forty-six years, and you will raise it up in three days?

(Jewish Persons 1 and 2 walk away, shaking heads.)

Narrator   Jesus was speaking about the temple of his body. When he was raised from the dead, his disciples remembered that he had said this. They came to believe the Scriptures and the words Jesus had spoken.
The Jewish temple was a sacred place. Our church building is holy, for it is the house of God. We speak and act in it with reverence.

Leader's Guide

Background Notes:

Jesus points to keeping the law as the way to enter the kingdom and have eternal life. In addition, in Mark's gospel Jesus demands that his followers give away their possessions to be saved. In Matthew, such extreme renunciation is not a mandate but a counsel of perfection for all people. In either case, Jesus reverses the Jewish concept that wealth is a sign of God's favor. It is a radical following of Jesus—the total commitment of heart and soul—that is the way of salvation. We must find our security in Jesus and not in possessions. The motivation behind giving up possessions is not because they are evil, or that asceticism has value, but that we must show concern for the poor.

To illustrate how nearly impossible it is for the rich to enter heaven, Jesus poses a humorous comparison, an oriental exaggeration. He says it is like a camel, the largest animal in Palestine, passing through the eye of a needle. While riches can be used to perform much good, they can be spiritually dangerous. Crime might be involved in attaining them. They can distract us from developing our spiritual life and relationship with God. They can cut us off from other people. They might even lead to exploiting others.

The rich will have a difficult time giving their possessions to the poor, but God can assist them. For the rich young man, it is too difficult. He is the only person in the gospels who refuses to follow Jesus. He does not respond to Jesus' love. His riches possess him.

Times for Use: Lessons on discipleship, holiness, riches, the kingdom, vocations.

QUESTIONS FOR CHILDREN

Before the play: Would you like to be wealthy? Why? Why might someone who is rich have a hard time following Jesus?

After the play: What prevented the young man from following Jesus? How did Jesus feel about him? How can we can be prevented from following Jesus? In what ways can we help the poor?

CLASS PRAYER

Take, Lord, and receive all my liberty,
my memory, my understanding, and my entire will.
Whatever I have and possess,
you have given to me.
To you, Lord, I now return it.
All is yours.
Dispose of it according to your will.
Give me only your love and your grace.
I will be rich enough; that is enough for me.
  —St. Ignatius of Loyola

CAST

Narrator
Jesus
Rich Man
Disciples 1, 2+

The Rich Young Man

MARK 10:17–31 MATTHEW 19:16–26 LUKE 18:18–27

(Jesus and Disciples 1, 2 walk along. Rich Man enters, runs up to Jesus and kneels before him.)

Rich Man   Good teacher, what must I do to inherit eternal life?

Jesus   Why do you call me good? No one is good but God alone. You know the commandments: "You shall not kill. You shall not commit adultery. You shall not steal. You shall not bear false witness. You shall not defraud. Honor your father and mother."

Rich Man   Teacher, I have kept all these from my youth.

(Jesus, looking at him lovingly, bends over and puts his hand on his shoulder.)

Jesus   You lack one thing. Go, sell what you own, and give the money to the poor, and you will have treasure in heaven. Then come, follow me.

(Rich Man lowers his head, shaking it. He rises and walks away from Jesus. Jesus watches sadly.)

Jesus   (looking around at Disciples) How hard it is for those who have wealth to enter the kingdom of God.

(Disciple 1 and Disciple 2 look shocked and puzzled.)

Jesus   Children, how hard it is to enter the kingdom of God. It is easier for a camel to go through the eye of a needle than for someone who is rich to enter the kingdom of God.

Disciple 1   (to Disciple 2) Then who can be saved?

Jesus   For human beings it is impossible, but not for God.

Narrator   Let's not allow anything to keep us away from Jesus: not wealth, other people, pride, laziness, or our sins.

Leader's Guide

THE WITHERED FIG TREE

Background Notes:

In Matthew the tree withered immediately after Jesus' curse. In Mark the disciples find it withered the next day. Mark notes that it was not the time for figs. Jesus appears irrational in demanding fruit out of season. Some scholars explain that Jesus was really looking for the edible, nut-shaped knobs that appeared before the leaves. If there were no knobs, there would be no fruit.

In the Old Testament a tree stands for life, and figs, a very sweet fruit, stand for blessedness and fulfillment. The story is a parable-in-action. The withered tree might symbolize Israel whose piety was mere lip-service and produced no good deeds. Many Israelites did not heed the prophets' warnings to change their hearts. Many Israelites did not respond to the message of Jesus. They were failures. On the other hand, the tree might stand for the end of the Temple and its worship.

The tree is barren when Jesus is in need of it. The purpose of the tree is to bear fruit. This story recalls the parable of the Barren Fig Tree, in which the owner threatens to cast his barren tree into the fire. Other gospel references to fruit are: "Every good tree bears good fruit" (Matthew 7:17) and "By their fruits you will know them" (Matthew 7:20).

Jesus' action leads into a discussion of faith and prayer. His warning to Israel ends with words of hope. It's not too late to change.

Times for Use: Lent, lessons on prayer, faith, holiness.

CAST	PROPS
Narrator	**Fig tree**
Jesus	**Withered fig tree**
Peter	
Disciples 1, 2+	

QUESTIONS FOR CHILDREN

Before the play: What would you do if you had an apple orchard and one of your trees didn't bear any apples? What kind of "good fruit" are we human beings supposed to bear?

After the play: How can you help yourself bear good fruit? How will prayer help you? What kinds of prayer can you pray?

CLASS PRAYER

O Lord, you who are all merciful,
take away my sins from me,
and enkindle within me the fire of your Holy Spirit.
Take away this heart of stone from me,
and give me a heart of flesh and blood,
a heart to love and adore you,
a heart which may delight in you,
love you and please you,
for Christ's sake.
    —St. Ambrose

The Withered Fig Tree

(Jesus, Peter, and Disciples walk along.)

Narrator   One day Jesus and his disciples were leaving Bethany.

Jesus   I'm hungry. Ah, I see a fig tree.

(Jesus leaves Disciples and goes on ahead to the fig tree. He looks for figs.)

Jesus   There's nothing here but leaves. No fruit.

Disciples 1   (to Disciple 2) But it's not the season for figs.

Jesus   (pointing to tree) May no one ever eat of your fruit again!

(Jesus and Disciples exit.)

Narrator   Leaving Jerusalem early in the morning, Jesus and the disciples were walking along.

(Jesus and Disciples enter.)

Peter   (excitedly) Rabbi, look! The fig tree that you cursed has withered away to its roots.

Jesus   Have faith in God. Truly I tell you, if you say to this mountain, (gestures to the right) "Be lifted up and thrown into the sea," and you do not doubt in your heart but believe that what you say will happen, it will be done for you. I tell you, all that you ask for in prayer, (folds hands) believe that you will receive it and it will be yours.
When you stand praying, forgive anyone who has hurt you, so that your Father in heaven (points up) may also forgive you your sins.

Narrator   We can be good trees that bear good fruit if we pray, for then we have God's help.

Leader's Guide

THE SAMARITAN WOMAN

Background Notes:
Jesus' conversation with the Samaritan woman was unconventional on several counts. First, she was a woman, and Jewish men didn't speak to women in public. Second, she was a Samaritan. The Samaritans were enemies of the Jewish people for two main reasons. First, during the Exile they had remained and had had intermarried with their foreign neighbors. Second, they worshiped in their own temple on Mount Gerizim instead of in Jerusalem. (When the Samaritans' offer to help rebuild the Temple in Jerusalem had been rejected, they built their own temple.) Usually, the Jewish people avoided passing through their territory, which lay between Judea and Galilee. It was surprising, too, that Jesus asks the woman for water since, according to Jewish Law, Samaritan utensils for eating and drinking were ritually unclean.

Jesus offers the woman living water, the Spirit released by the crucified and risen Jesus, the gift that confers eternal life. Christians receive this gift through the waters of Baptism. As they converse, the woman constantly misinterprets Jesus' messages but comes to recognize him as prophet and eventually Messiah. He affirms that he is the Messiah by stating, "I am he." The "I am" indicates divinity. It recalls the name Yahweh revealed to Moses: "I am who am." Then the Samaritan woman becomes the first missionary. She spreads the news about Jesus to her neighbors. They learn for themselves that Jesus is the Savior of the world. At the well, a Jewish place of courtship, Jesus replaces the five husbands in the woman's life.

Times for Use: Lessons on the identity of Jesus, the mission of Jesus, women, evangelization.

CAST — PROPS

CAST	PROPS
Narrator	Pail or water jar
Jesus	Package (for food)
Disciples 1, 2+	Chair
Woman	
Samaritans 1, 2+	

QUESTIONS FOR CHILDREN

Before the play: What do we use water for? Why is it a good symbol for the Holy Spirit?

After the play: What was unusual about what Jesus did? What was the living water he offered the woman? How did her neighbors come to believe in Jesus? How can we come to know him better?

CLASS PRAYER

Carry out this prayer activity:

• Pour water from a glass pitcher into a glass in front of your students.

• Have the students recall how good cool water tastes when they are hot and thirsty. Ask them to think back to a time when water tasted really good to them.

• Invite them to close their eyes and imagine that they are like an empty cup. God can fill them up with powerful divine life, with divine love. They can be refreshed and renewed.

• Suggest that they repeat over and over in their hearts: "My soul thirsts for God, for the living God" (Psalm 42:2). Allow at least a minute for this.

The Samaritan Woman

JOHN 4:4–42

Narrator	Passing through Samaria, Jesus and the disciples came to a town called Sychar. It was near the land Jacob had given to his son Joseph. Jacob's well was there. The Jewish people and the Samaritans did not get along. They would have nothing to do with one another.
	(Jesus and Disciples enter. Jesus goes to chair and sits.)
Jesus	I'm tired from this journey. Let me sit a while here at Jacob's well.
Disciple 1	Sure, Master. It's about noon. We'll go into town and buy some food. (to other Disciples) Come on.
	(Disciples exit. Woman enters with pail and goes to where Jesus is.)
Jesus	Give me a drink.
Woman	(surprised) How is it that you, a Jew, ask a drink of me, a Samaritan woman?
Jesus	If you knew the gift of God and who it is that is saying to you, "Give me a drink," you would have asked him, and he would have given you living water.
Woman	Sir, you have no bucket, and the well is deep. Where then can you get this living water? Are you greater than our ancestor Jacob, who gave us the well and with his children and his flocks drank from it?
Jesus	Everyone who drinks this water (points to well) will be thirsty again. But whoever drinks the water that I will give them will never be thirsty. The water that I will give will become in them a spring of water gushing up to eternal life.
Woman	Sir, give me this water, so that I may never be thirsty or have to keep coming here to draw water.
Jesus	(gestures to town) Go, call your husband, and come back.
Woman	I do not have a husband.
Jesus	You are right in saying, "I have no husband." For you have had five husbands, (holds up hand with fingers spread) and the one you have now is not your husband. What you have said is true!
Woman	Sir, I see that you are a prophet. Our ancestors worshiped on this mountain. But

your people say that the place to worship is in Jerusalem.

Jesus   (stands) Believe me, woman, the hour is coming when you will worship the Father neither on this mountain (points down) nor in Jerusalem (points in distance). Your people worship what you do not know. We worship what we know, because salvation is from the Jews.
But the hour is coming, and is now here, when the true worshipers will worship the Father in spirit and truth (puts hand over heart). The Father seeks such people to worship him. God is spirit, and those who worship him must worship in Spirit and truth.

Woman   I know that the Messiah is coming, the one called the Anointed. When he comes, he will tell us everything.

Jesus   (points to self) I am he, the one who is speaking to you.

(Disciples enter with package.)

Disciple 1   (to Disciple 2) Look. Jesus is talking to a woman.

Disciple 2   I don't believe my eyes!

(Woman exits, leaving her pail.)

Disciple 1   (handing package to Jesus) Rabbi, eat something.

Jesus   I have food to eat that you do not know about.

Disciple 2   (to Disciple 3) Could someone have brought him something to eat?

Jesus   My food is to do the will of the one who sent me and to complete his work.

(Jesus opens package. He and Disciples sit down on the ground. Woman enters with Persons 1, 2)

Woman   (to Persons 1, 2) I'm sure he is the Messiah. He told me everything I have done.

Person 1   I believe you.

Person 2   I'll soon see if what you say is true.

(Woman and Persons 1, 2 go to Jesus.)

Woman	Rabbi, these are my neighbors.
Jesus	Glad to meet you.
Person 1	Won't you stay with us a while?
Jesus	I'd be happy to.

(All exit.)

Narrator	Jesus stayed with the Samaritans two days. Many more came to believe in him.

(All enter.)

Person 2	Jesus, we hate to see you go.
Person 1	Come again.
Jesus and Disciples	We'll try. So long. Thanks for everything.

(Jesus and Disciples exit, waving to Woman and Persons.)

Person 1	(to Woman) We no longer believe because of your word.
Person 2	We have heard for ourselves and we know that this is truly the Savior of the world.
Narrator	Jesus offers us living water too. We accept it whenever we celebrate the sacraments. Then we are empowered to go out and bring others to him.

Leader's Guide

Background Notes:

The story of the Pardon of the Sinful Woman in Luke's gospel is very similar to the story of the Anointing at Bethany in the other gospels. The main difference is that the woman in Luke's story is a sinner who has been forgiven by Jesus.

Jesus is dining at the home of Simon, a Pharisee. He is probably reclining on a mat at a low table with his sandals off. A woman who is known to be a sinner comes to anoint Jesus' feet. She bursts into tears, then dries his feet with her hair and anoints them.

Simon thinks to himself that Jesus is no prophet or he would not let the woman touch him. Then Jesus shows himself a prophet by reading Simon's mind. He explains that the woman has been forgiven, and she has shown more love than Simon himself. Simon could have shown Jesus these special courtesies performed for a guest: a kiss of greeting, water for his feet, and oil for his head. Simon's stinginess is in sharp contrast to the woman's generosity.

Jesus tells a parable that illustrates how a person who has been forgiven more, loves more. Jesus forgives the woman and gives her peace. The self-righteous Simon learns a lesson.

Times for Use: Before the sacrament of reconciliation, lessons on forgiveness, the mission of Jesus, conversion, love, women, sinners, hypocrisy.

QUESTIONS FOR CHILDREN

Before the play: How do you feel after you've done something wrong? What can you do to make up?

After the play: How was the woman different from Simon? How did she show love for Jesus? How do the steps of the Sacrament of Reconciliation help us toward conversion? How can we show love for Jesus?

CLASS PRAYER

Lead the students to reflect on God's forgiveness:

Recall God's great love in forgiving our human race. After creating Adam and Eve, God endured the rejection of his friendship. Still God reached out to us and gave us a second chance. Through Jesus and his death and resurrection we can once again be God's children. We can have the gift of divine life and live forever. [Pause.]

Recall God's love in forgiving you just as he forgave the sinful woman. Think back at the times you have sinned and have not done as God wished. [Pause.] As soon as you were sorry, God has offered you forgiveness. Time and again God forgave you for little sins and perhaps for big sins. Maybe God has forgiven you every day. Maybe God has forgiven you over and over for the same sins. No one can fathom the depths of God's mercy and great love. Spend some time now thanking God in your heart for being so good and for forgiving us repeatedly. [Pause.]

You might ask God now for the grace to show your love in return by avoiding sin. [Pause.] Whenever you do sin, you can trust that God loves you and will always accept you back. Ask for the wisdom to return to God immediately. [Pause.]

CAST	PROPS
Narrator	Table and four chairs
Jesus	Plates
Simon	Flask for ointment
Persons 1, 2+	
Woman	

The Pardon of the Sinful Woman

LUKE 7:36–50

(Table and chairs are in the center. Simon and Persons 1, 2 are seated.)

Narrator Once a Pharisee named Simon invited Jesus to dine with him.

(Jesus enters and goes to Simon.)

Jesus Hello, Simon.

Simon Jesus! I'm so glad you came. Welcome to my table.

(Jesus sits with his feet tucked behind him.)

Simon (offering Jesus a plate) Here, have some of this fresh bread.

Narrator Now there was a sinful woman in the city who learned that Jesus was at table in the house of the Pharisee. She came with an alabaster flask of ointment.

(Woman enters with flask, goes behind Jesus, and weeps.)

Simon Hey, you're getting his feet wet.

(Woman stoops and pretends to wipe Jesus' feet with her hair and kiss them.)

Person 1 (with shocked expression to Person 2) She's wiping his feet with her hair.

Person 2 And kissing them.

(Woman pretends to pour the ointment on his feet.)

Simon (aside) If this man were a prophet, he would know what kind of woman this is who is touching him. She is a sinner.

Jesus Simon, I have something to say to you.

Simon Teacher, speak.

Jesus Two people were in debt to a certain man. One owed five hundred days' wages, and the other owed fifty. When they could not repay him, he cancelled the debts for both of them. Now which of them will love him more?

Simon I suppose the one for whom he cancelled the greater debt.

Jesus	You have judged rightly. (turning and gesturing to Woman) Do you see this woman? When I entered your house, you gave me no water for my feet, but she has bathed them with her tears and dried them with her hair. You did not give me a kiss, but since the time I came in, she has not stopped kissing my feet. You did not anoint my head with oil (gestures toward head), but she has anointed my feet with ointment (gestures toward feet).
	Therefore, I tell you, her many sins have been forgiven, so she has shown great love. But the one to whom little is forgiven loves little. (to Woman) Your sins are forgiven.
Person 1	(to Person 2) Who is this who even forgives sins?
Jesus	(to Woman) Your faith has saved you. Go in peace.
	(Woman exits, walking backwards looking at Jesus.)
Narrator	God is always willing to forgive us. May we pray an act of contrition after we sin and celebrate the sacrament of reconciliation regularly. Then we will experience God's love in a new way.

Leader's Guide

Background Notes:
The details of this event differ from gospel to gospel. In Matthew and Mark, Jesus' head is anointed. It was the custom to anoint the heads of guests. In John, Jesus' feet are anointed. Matthew and Mark identify the host as Simon the leper. John identifies the woman as Mary, the sister of Lazarus and Judas as the disciple who complains.

The perfume the woman uses, which is made from a rare Indian plant, is valued at three hundred days' wages. It was sealed in an alabaster vase in such a way that the fragrance would be kept in. The vase had to be broken before the perfume could be used. Perhaps the woman strikes it on the edge of the table. Jesus shows appreciation for the woman's generous gesture and defends it. He states that it will always be remembered (and it has been so far). This occurs in an age when women's actions were unnoticed, unrewarded, and unrecorded.

Jesus asserts that he will not always be there, whereas the poor will. And he describes the anointing as prophetic—a preparation for his burial. Bodies were anointed with spices and oil before being buried. Jesus never was anointed. His burial was hurried, and when the women did come to anoint him, he was already risen.

In Matthew and Mark the anointing occurs after the chief priests and elders have conspired to arrest Jesus and before Judas arranged the betrayal with them. The woman's extravagant act of love softens the unfolding of the tragic events that led to the end of Jesus' life, when his blood was poured out for us in another extravagant act of love.

Times for Use: Lessons on love for Jesus, the death of Jesus.

CAST

Narrator
Jesus
Simon
Persons 1, 2+
Woman

PROPS

Table and chairs
Jar

QUESTIONS FOR CHILDREN

Before the play: Did anyone ever laugh at you for doing something that was Christian? What are some things that Christians do or believe today that others might consider foolish?

After the play: How was the woman's gesture a great act of love? How was she different from Judas? What can we do to honor Jesus? When is anointing used in the church today? Why?

CLASS PRAYER

Invite the students to think of one special way they can show love for Jesus soon. It may be saying a certain prayer tonight, volunteering somewhere, or doing something difficult for love of him such as acting to change a bad habit. You might discuss ideas and then allow several moments for the students to decide what they wish to do. End by praying together the traditional Act of Love:

O my God, I love you above all things,
with my whole whole heart and soul
because you are all-good and worthy of all my love.
I love my neighbor as myself for the love of you.
I forgive all who have injured me,
and I ask pardon of all whom I have injured. Amen.

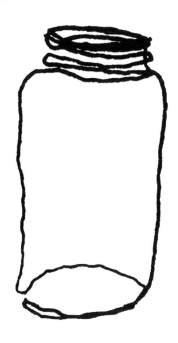

The Anointing at Bethany

MATTHEW 26:6–13   MARK 14:3–9   JOHN 12:1–8

(Jesus, Simon, and Persons 1, 2 are seated at table.)

Narrator   One day Jesus was at table in the house of Simon the leper in Bethany. A woman came with an alabaster jar of costly perfumed oil.

(Woman enters. She "breaks" the top off the jar by hitting it against the table and "pours" the contents on Jesus' head.)

Person 1   (angrily) What a stupid thing to do!

Person 2   (to Woman) Why this waste of perfumed oil?

Person 1   It could have been sold for more than three hundred days' wages.

Person 2   And the money given to the poor.

Jesus   (puts up hand) Let her alone. Why do you make trouble for her? She has performed a good service for me. The poor you will always have with you. You can show kindness to them whenever you wish. But you will not always have me. (gesturing toward Woman) She has done what she could. By pouring this perfume on my body, she has prepared me for burial.
Truly I tell you, wherever the gospel is proclaimed in the whole world (gestures widely), what she has done will be told in memory of her.

Narrator   The fragrance of the perfume filled the house. And Jesus' words came true. We all know the story of the woman's beautiful act of love. May we imitate her overwhelming show of love for Jesus by serving him and his people.

Leader's Guide

PETER'S PROFESSION OF FAITH

Background Notes:

Although the account begins with what people think of Jesus, the focus is what the apostles think of him. Peter, as usual, is their spokesperson. While others, including King Herod, say that Jesus is a prophet returned to earth, Peter proclaims that Jesus is the Messiah, the fulfillment of the Old Testament promises. Peter is the first person to do so. He does not know Jesus' identity on his own. This knowledge is a gift from God. In response, Jesus declares that his church will be founded on Peter, whose name means "rock." The powers of death shall not overcome the church. Keys symbolize power. They open and close, admit or exclude. Jesus bestows on Peter and his successors the power to lead the church until the end of time. Whatever they declare lawful will be held lawful in heaven.

Jesus' warning not to tell others is interpreted in different ways. It could be that he did not want people to follow him as the kind of Messiah they expected—a powerful worldly ruler who frees them from their oppressors. In Matthew's account, Peter adds that Jesus is the Son of the living God.

Times for Use: Lessons on faith, the identity of Jesus, Peter, the church.

CAST

Narrator
Jesus
Peter
Disciples 1, 2, 3+

QUESTIONS FOR CHILDREN

Before the play: Who do you believe Jesus is? Why was it hard for the Israelites to accept Jesus as their Messiah?

After the play: What special role do Peter and the popes have in the church? In what ways is the present pope guiding the church? How is our bishop guiding it?

CLASS PRAYER

Pray a litany for the church as below. The students may add petitions.

Response: Pray for us.
St. Peter,…
Apostles, first leaders of the church,…
All saintly popes and bishops,…
Mary, Mother of the Church,…

Response: Hear us, O Lord.
That our Holy Father, Pope (Name), may be a good shepherd of the church,…
That our church leaders may have the wisdom and courage to guide us well,…
That the bishop of our diocese, Bishop (Name), may lead us with love,…
That our pope and bishops may have good health and strength to carry out their responsibilities,…
That they may be filled with the gifts of the Holy Spirit, to serve as Jesus did,…
That under their leadership, the church may flourish and faith grow strong,…
That all believers may come to unity,…

Let us pray. Lord, you have given us leaders to guide us to holiness and to you. We believe that through them you act in the world and lead us. Give them the grace always to be true to you, and give us the grace to be open to their teachings. Amen.

Peter's Profession of Faith

MATTHEW 16:13–20 MARK 8:27–30 LUKE 9:18–21

(Jesus, Peter, and Disciples 1, 2, 3 walk along.)

Jesus Who do people say that the Son of Man is?

Disciple 1 Some say John the Baptist.

Disciple 2 Others, Elijah.

Disciple 3 And still others Jeremiah or one of the prophets.

(Jesus stops walking and faces the Disciples and Peter.)

Jesus (pointing to Disciples) But who do you say that I am?

Peter You are the Messiah, the Son of the living God.

(Jesus puts his hand on Peter's shoulder.)

Jesus (to Peter) Blessed are you, Simon son of John! For flesh and blood has not revealed this to you, but my Father in heaven.
And I tell you, you are Peter, and on this rock I will build my church, and the gates of the underworld will not prevail against it.
I will give you the keys of the kingdom of heaven. Whatever you bind on earth (points down with right hand) will be bound in heaven (points up); and whatever you loose on earth (points down with left hand) will be loosed in heaven (points up).

Jesus (looking around at the Disciples) Now I give you strict orders: Don't tell anyone that I am the Messiah. The Son of Man must undergo great suffering, and be rejected by the elders, chief priests, and scribes, and be killed, and on the third day be raised.

Narrator Peter became the head of the church. He followed Jesus and led the early church until, like his master, he was killed on a cross. Who is Jesus for you? Do you respond to him as though he were your Messiah, the living God?

Leader's Guide

Background Notes:

At the Transfiguration, Jesus is revealed in glory to Peter, James, and John, the three apostles privileged to be alone with him on other occasions. The Transfiguration anticipates the resurrection glory of Jesus and confirms his messiahship. The account is rooted in some mystical experience the three disciples had. They did not perceive the impact of it until after the resurrection. The expression "six days" links the event to Peter's confession of faith at Caesarea Philippi. The high mountain is traditionally held to be Mount Tabor.

Details of the story that are reminiscent of God's theophany on Sinai point to Jesus as the New Moses: the high mountain, the cloud, Moses' presence, and the tents. The apostles represent the new people of God. Moses and Elijah, who are present at the event, stand for the Law and the prophets. As such, they witness to Jesus. He is the fulfillment of the Law and the greatest prophet. They discuss Jesus' fate—that he is to suffer and die. The cloud and the mountain symbolize God's presence, and Jesus' dazzling appearance signifies the divine world. Tents were used during the Exodus. Peter's suggestion to make tents could refer to this journey to freedom or simply reflect his wish to prolong the experience.

The apostles fall to the ground in fear. They do not understand. The words of the Father confirm Jesus' role as the Messiah and reveal his divine sonship. The Transfiguration may have been intended to strengthen the apostles' faith during the passion and death of Jesus.

Times for Use: Lessons on the identity of Jesus, the suffering of Jesus, the Resurrection.

QUESTIONS FOR CHILDREN

Before the play: At what times in the gospels was it shown that Jesus was God? When Jesus was put to death, why might his followers have doubted that he was God?

After the play: How does the Transfiguration story parallel that of Moses at Mount Sinai? Why do you think the Transfiguration took place? How do we regard the suffering and death of Jesus?

CLASS PRAYER

O most merciful Redeemer,
friend and brother,
may we know you more clearly,
love you more dearly,
and follow you more nearly,
for your own sake.
    —St. Richard of Chichester

CAST   PROPS

Narrator   Cloud
Jesus
Peter
James
John
Moses
Elijah
Voice

The Transfiguration of Jesus

MATTHEW 17:1–8 MARK 9:2–8 LUKE 9:28–36

(Jesus, Peter, James, and John enter.)

Jesus (gesturing up) My three friends, come up this mountain with me.

(Jesus, Peter, James, and John walk around with difficulty as if climbing.)

Narrator Jesus and the three apostles went up the high mountain by themselves. As Jesus prayed, he was transfigured before them.

(Jesus extends his arms. Peter, James, and John kneel and shade their eyes.)

Narrator The face of Jesus shone like the sun, and his clothes became dazzling white. Moses and Elijah appeared.

(Moses and Elijah enter and go to Jesus, one on each side.)

Narrator Moses and Elijah talked to Jesus. They spoke about the passion and death he would undergo in Jerusalem.

Peter Lord, it is good for us to be here. If you wish, I will make three tents here, one for you, one for Moses, and one for Elijah.

Narrator While Peter was still speaking, a bright cloud cast a shadow over them. From the cloud came a voice.

Voice (loud and strong) This is my beloved Son, with him I am well pleased. Listen to him!

(Peter, James, and John fall to the ground face down and tremble. Jesus walks over to them and touches each one.)

Jesus Get up and do not be afraid.

(Peter, James, and John sit up, open their eyes, and rub them. They look around.)

Narrator They saw no one else but Jesus.

Jesus Let's go down now.

(Jesus, Peter, James, and John walk around.)

Jesus   Tell no one about the vision until after the Son of Man has been raised from the dead.

Narrator   Jesus is God. Let us adore him, pray to him, make sacrifices for him, and obey him. Someday we will live with him forever.

Leader's Guide

Background Notes:

Martha, Mary, and their brother Lazarus lived in Bethany, a town near Jerusalem. Jesus often visited these good friends.

This story illustrates the primary place of faith in the life of a Christian. Martha invites Jesus to her house but then is totally absorbed in the task of serving him and his companions. Meanwhile Mary, her sister, sits at the Lord's feet, listening to his teaching. This is the posture of a disciple took while being taught by the master. It is unusual that a woman would assume this posture. When Martha complains to Jesus that he apparently isn't noticing that she is doing all the work, Jesus chides Martha for her busy-ness, her anxiety, and worry. Perhaps she was doing more than was necessary. Jesus teaches that focusing on him, as Mary is doing, is not only good but necessary. Valuing the person of Jesus and his message is the only thing that matters. However, we must balance prayer with love in action.

Times for Use: Lessons on faith, love for Jesus, prayer, Christian life.

QUESTIONS FOR CHILDREN

Before the play: Who were some of Jesus' friends? How do you show you are a friend of Jesus?

After the play: Why did Jesus praise Mary? Why is it important to pray? How do we serve Jesus today? What do you think happened at the end of this story?

CLASS PRAYER

Dear Jesus,
help us to spread your fragrance everywhere.
Flood our souls with your spirit and life.
Penetrate and possess our whole being so utterly
that our lives may be only a radiance of yours.
Let us thus praise you in the way you love best:
by shining on those around us.
Let us preach you without preaching,
not by words, but by our example
by the catching force,
the influence of what we do,
the evident fullness of the love our hearts bear to you.
—adapted from John Henry Cardinal Newman's prayer

CAST	PROPS
Narrator	Large pot and ladle
Jesus	Dishes
Disciples 1, 2+	Table
Martha	Chairs for Jesus
Mary	and Disciples

Martha and Mary

LUKE 10:38–42

(Martha stands in the center of the stage in front of chairs. Mary is in the background. Pot is on the floor, and dishes on the table. Jesus and Disciples enter.)

Jesus   Martha! How are you?

Martha   (excitedly) Jesus! I'm fine. Welcome to Bethany. Dinner is almost ready. Won't you join us?

Jesus   I'd love to.

Martha   Come in.

Mary   (going to Jesus) Master, it's so good to see you!

(Jesus and Disciples are seated. Mary sits at Jesus' feet. Martha goes to pot and stirs.)

Mary   What have you been doing, Jesus?

Jesus   We've been teaching in towns as we journey to Jerusalem.

(Martha sets table.)

Mary   Tell me. What did you teach at the last town you were in?

Jesus   Well, someone asked me what to do to have eternal life…

(Martha walks over to Jesus.)

Martha   (hands on hips) Lord, do you not care that my sister has left me to do all the work by myself? Tell her then to help me.

Jesus   (shaking head) Martha, Martha, you are worried and distracted by many things. There is need of only one thing. Mary has chosen the better part, which will not be taken away from her.

Narrator   Following Jesus means both serving him by acts of love and being with him in prayer.

Leader's Guide

Background Notes:

The Pharisees seek to trap Jesus in the matter of paying taxes. Beginning in 6 A.D., the Romans exacted from the Jewish people a census tax, which the Jewish people resented. The tax had to be paid by a silver Roman coin. If Jesus supported the tax, he would alienate his people. If he said the tax shouldn't be paid, his enemies could report him to the governor as a rebel, like a Zealot. Jesus escapes the trap by using his wit. Coins bore the image of the emperor and were inscribed "Tiberius Caesar, son of the divine Augustus." They were his possession. Ironically, when Jesus asks for this coin, the Pharisees have one, though apparently Jesus does not. This means they already submit to the emperor themselves and use his system of commerce.

By saying, "Give to Caesar the things that are Caesar's and to God the things that are God's," Jesus implies that loyalty to state and obedience to God need not contradict. It is up to us to apply this principle and determine what exactly belongs to "Caesar."

Times for Use: Lessons on obedience, the fourth commandment.

QUESTIONS FOR CHILDREN

Before the play: What are some laws and rules that you follow? Why do you try to keep them? Why do your parents pay taxes?

After the play: How did the Pharisees try to get Jesus into trouble this time? Why were they always trying to trap Jesus? What do we owe God? What do we owe the government?

CLASS PRAYER

Lord, help us give every person what he or she deserves. May we give our parents obedience and those who care for us respect. May we give our religious leaders reverence. May we give our friends truthfulness and joy and our neighbors honesty and assistance. May we give the poor kindness and compassion. Above all, may we give you praise, glory, and love forever.

CAST

Narrator
Jesus
Pharisees 1, 2+
Pharisees'
  Disciples 1, 2+
Crowd

PROPS

Money bag
Coin

Paying Taxes to Caesar

MATTHEW 22:15–22 MARK 12:13–17 LUKE 20:20–26

(Pharisees enter. Pharisees' Disciples follow at a distance.)

Pharisee 1   (to Pharisee 2) We must trap him in his speech.

Pharisee 2   Yes. If we make him look like a fool, his followers will leave him.

Pharisee 1   If we can get him to speak against the government, we might be rid of him.

Pharisee   I've got it. (to Pharisees' Disciples) Come here.

(Pharisees' Disciples walk up to Pharisees 1, 2.)

Pharisee 2   Find Jesus. Ask him if it is lawful to pay taxes to Caesar. (laughs wickedly) That'll stump him.

(Pharisees 1, 2 exit laughing. Jesus and Crowd enter. Pharisees' Disciples go to Jesus.)

Pharisees' Disciple 1   Ah, Teacher, we know that you are a truthful man and that you teach the way of God in accordance with truth.

Pharisees' Disciple 2   And you are not concerned with anyone's opinion, for you do not regard a person's status.

Pharisees' Disciple 1   Tell us, then, what do you think: Is it lawful to pay the census tax to Caesar or not?

Pharisees' Disciple 2   Should we pay or should we not pay?

(Jesus gives them a hard look.)

Jesus   Why are you testing me, you hypocrites? Show me the coin that pays the census tax.

(Pharisees' Disciple 1 opens his money bag and takes out a coin.)

Pharisees' Disciple 1   (handing coin to Jesus) Here. A Roman coin.

Jesus   (holding up coin) Whose image is this and whose inscription?

Pharisees'
Disciples 1,2 Caesar's.

Jesus   (calmly) Then repay to Caesar what belongs to Caesar and to God what belongs to God.

        (Pharisees' Disciples 1, 2 gasp. They turn and walk away quickly.)

Narrator   Jesus wants us to obey rightful authority: our parents, teachers, policemen, and anyone else set over us to care for us. We owe them obedience, honor, and gratitude.

Leader's Guide

Background Notes:
The Pharisees use a woman's humiliation to try to ensnare Jesus. Having caught her in adultery, they bring her to him and ask if she should be stoned. If Jesus answers "No," he will be contradicting the Law of Moses which prescribes death for her crime. If Jesus answers "Yes," he will depart from his own teaching of mercy. Jesus writes on the ground. What he writes and why remain a mystery. One theory is that Jesus was listing the sins of all those present.

Then Jesus cleverly invites those without sin to throw the first stone. Conscious of their sins and perhaps realizing how base was the trap they laid, the Pharisees disperse. In St. Augustine's words, "There remained together great misery and great mercy." Jesus, the sinless one, frees the woman but with an admonition to sin no more. He gives her a chance to change her life.

Times for Use: Before the sacrament of reconciliation, lessons on forgiveness, sinners, hypocrisy.

CAST   PROPS

Narrator   **Chair**
Jesus
Woman
Scribes 1, 2+
Pharisees 1, 2+
Crowd+

QUESTIONS FOR CHILDREN

Before the play: How do you feel when you are caught doing something wrong? How do you feel when you are forgiven? Is there anyone who doesn't need to be forgiven sometime?

After the play: What do you think Jesus wrote on the ground? Why? Why should we forgive others? How do we show we forgive others? How are Christians forgiven?

CLASS PRAYER

Ask the students to think of the sin they are most sorry for. Remind them that Jesus is just as willing to forgive them as he was the woman who had sinned. His mercy is without bounds. So is his love for us. Pray an act of contrition together. You can use the traditional formula, the formula in the new Rite of Penance, or one that you compose.

The Woman Caught in Adultery

JOHN 8:2–11

Narrator	Early one morning Jesus walked in the temple area.
	(Jesus enters. Crowd enters gradually. Jesus sits.)
Jesus	I am the light of the world. Whoever follows me will not walk in darkness…
Narrator	Jesus was interrupted when some scribes and Pharisees brought a woman to him. She had been caught in adultery.
	(Scribes and Pharisees enter with Woman. Pharisee 1 and Pharisee 2 are on either side of her.)
Pharisee 1	(pointing to ground before Jesus, to Woman) Stand there in the middle.
	(Woman stands before Jesus with her head down.)
Pharisee 2	Teacher, this woman was caught in the very act of committing adultery.
Scribe 1	Now in the law, Moses commanded us to stone such women.
Scribe 2	So what do you say?
Narrator	They said this to test him, so that they could have some charge to bring against him.
	(Jesus stoops and writes with his finger on the ground.)
Pharisee 1	Well, Jesus, what do you say?
Pharisee 2	Do we stone her or not?
	(Jesus straightens up.)
Jesus	(looking around at them) Let the one among you who is without sin be the first to throw a stone at her.
	(Jesus stoops again and writes on the ground. Scribes and Pharisees look at writing. One by one they leave. When Jesus and Woman are alone, Jesus sit up.)
Jesus	Woman, where are they? Has no one condemned you?
Woman	No one, sir.

78

Jesus   Neither do I condemn you. Go, and from now on do not sin again.

(Woman walks away slowly, looking back at Jesus from time to time.)

Narrator   Jesus shows loving mercy for sinners. If we are Christians, people who are like Christ, we will have compassion on sinners too.

Leader's Guide

Background Notes:
Jesus demonstrates that it is possible for a rich man to be saved. Zacchaeus is a tax collector who collected taxes for the Roman oppressors. Tax collectors were allowed to keep for themselves any money collected above their quota. This practice led to greed and abuse of the people. To the Jewish people then, tax collector was synonymous with sinner.

Zacchaeus was short, so in order to see Jesus passing by, he climbs a sycamore tree—a tree with a short trunk and wide branches. This act took ingenuity and humility. When Jesus invites himself to Zacchaeus's house, the crowd objects. But Zacchaeus responds with joy. He is open to Jesus, and his life is changed. He makes restitution for his sins far beyond what is necessary. His whole household reaps the benefits. This story clearly shows that Jesus seeks out sinners. The good shepherd is always on the lookout for lost sheep.

Times for Use: Before the sacrament of reconciliation, lessons on conversion, forgiveness, the mission of Jesus.

QUESTIONS FOR CHILDREN

Before the play: What are some physical shortcomings people can have? What are some other kinds of shortcomings? Who are some people who were great despite their flaws?

After the play: How did Jesus reach out to Zacchaeus? How was Zacchaeus open to salvation? What did he do as signs of his conversion? In what ways does Jesus reach out to us?

CLASS PRAYER

Have mercy on me, O God.
  according to your steadfast love;
according to your abundant mercy
  blot out my sins.
Wash me thoroughly from my wickedness
  and cleanse me from my sin.
Create in me a clean heart, O God,
  and put a new and right spirit within me.
    —Psalm 51:1, 2, 10

CAST

CAST	PROPS
Narrator	Chair or ladder for tree
Jesus	
Zacchaeus	
Person	
Crowd+	

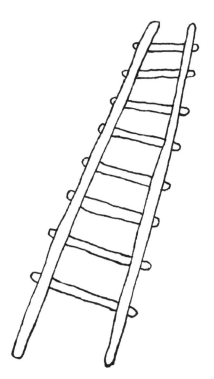

Zacchaeus, the Tax Collector

LUKE 19:1–10

(Crowd and Persons 1, 2 are on one side of stage facing the wings. Tree is on the other side. Zacchaeus stands between the Crowd and the tree.)

Narrator   Once Jesus was passing through the town of Jericho. Now a man there named Zacchaeus was a chief tax collector and a rich man. He was not liked because of his job. Zacchaeus wanted to see who Jesus was, but he could not see him because of the crowd. He was too short.

(Crowd looks off stage. Zacchaeus tries to look between people.)

Person 1   (excitedly) I see him! I see him! He's coming!

(Zacchaeus jumps up and down to see. He shakes his head and looks frustrated. He sees the tree, his face brightens, and he snaps his fingers. He runs to the tree and climbs up.)

Narrator   From the sycamore tree Zacchaeus had a good view of Jesus.

(Jesus enters and Crowd moves along with him toward the tree. At the tree Jesus looks up.)

Jesus   (shouting) Zacchaeus, hurry and come down, for I must stay at your house today.

(Zacchaeus climbs down.)

Zacchaeus   You don't mean it! How wonderful. I am honored. Come with me.

(Jesus and Zacchaeus begin to walk off.)

Person 2   (angrily) He has gone to stay at the house of a sinner.

(Zacchaeus stops.)

Zacchaeus   (to Jesus) Look, half of my possessions, Lord, I will give to the poor, and if I have stolen anything from anyone, I will pay back four times as much.

Jesus   (to Zacchaeus) Today salvation has come to his house because he too is a descendant of Abraham. For the Son of Man has come to seek and to save what is lost.

(Jesus and Zacchaeus walk off, Jesus' arm around Zacchaeus.)

Narrator   Jesus forgave Zacchaeus and made him a better man. Who knows what good we do when we forgive others who have hurt us on purpose or unintentionally?

Leader's Guide

Background Notes:

In the Temple's Court of Women were thirteen horn-shaped chests for offerings, each labeled for a certain purpose, such as incense, doves, and oil. Jesus sits and watches people deposit money. A widow comes. She is one of the truly holy Jewish people who contrast with the righteous "pious ones." The widow puts in two copper coins, the smallest coins in circulation. Jesus praises her generosity because the coins were all she had. She didn't even keep one of the two coins for herself. Her offering was more than everyone else's, for she gave her total security. She trusted God to care for her. The story of the widow's offering leads into the story of Christ's offering. He, too, gave his all.

Times for Use: Lent and lessons on the poor, generosity, holiness.

QUESTIONS FOR CHILDREN

Before the play: When do people contribute to the church? Do you use church envelopes? How much should we give to the church?

After the play: Why was the widow's offering great? Why do you think she was willing to give that much? What can we offer the church besides money?

CLASS PRAYER

Tell the students to take out a coin. Have pennies on hand in case students don't have change. Ask the students what they observe about the coin, for instance, its size, shape, weight, what is imprinted on it. Ask what the coin is used for. Then guide the students in the following reflection:

Each of us is like a coin that belongs to God. God made us, and we have value in God's eyes. Because God owns us, everything we are is for God's glory. Like money, our lives can be used in different ways. They can be used for good or for evil. Everything we do can be offered to God as a gift. We want to live in such a way that God is proud of us and happy that we are his. At the end of our lives we will return to God. Then we will realize whether our lives have been wasted or have been lived generously.

CAST

Narrator
Jesus
Disciples 1, 2+
Wealthy persons
  1, 2+
Widow

PROPS

Chair
Large bowl for money
Table for bowl
Bags of money
Two small coins

The Widow's Offering

MARK 12:41–44 LUKE 21:1–5

(Chair is opposite bowl. Jesus and Disciples 1, 2 enter. Jesus walks away and sits down.)

Narrator One day Jesus sat watching people put money into the temple treasury.

(Wealthy Person 1 enters, empties bag into bowl, and exits. Wealthy Person 2 enters, empties bag into bowl, and exits. Disciple 1 sees this.)

Disciple 1 (to Disciple 2) Wow! Did you see that? Those people just gave to the treasury more money than I've made all my life.

Narrator A poor widow came along with two small copper coins.

(Widow enters and shyly puts two coins in bowl. She exits.)

Jesus (to Disciples) Come here.

(Disciples go to Jesus.)

Jesus Truly I tell you, this poor widow has put in more than all the other contributors to the treasury. For all of them have contributed from their surplus wealth, but she, from her poverty, has offered all she had to live on.

Narrator We have an opportunity to give to God in church collections and collections for the poor and needy. We can be stingy, or we can be generous like the widow.

Leader's Guide

Background Notes:

Jesus enters Jerusalem as Messiah-king. Jerusalem was the holy city where the Temple was located. It was also King David's city. Jesus rides a colt, not a horse, because he is not a military Messiah but a humble one who comes in peace. The people who know about his raising Lazarus from the dead acclaim him as king and Messiah. They hope for the restoration of David's kingdom. They strew branches on the ground to make it soft. They spread their cloaks, the red carpet treatment afforded royalty. They greet Jesus with hosannas, a cry of acclamation that means "Do save us." The Pharisees fear that the procession might attract the notice of the Romans. But their attempts to quell the noisy crowd are futile. They admit that the whole world is following after Jesus.

Times for Use: Before Passion Sunday or the Feast of Christ the King, with lessons on the identity of Jesus, humility.

CAST	PROPS
Narrator	**Chair, broom or mop**
Jesus	**for colt**
Disciples	**Rope for colt**
1, 2, 3, 4+	**Cloaks**
Bystander	**Branches**
Crowd+	
Pharisees 1, 2	
Person+	

QUESTIONS FOR CHILDREN

Before the play: Do you have palm branches in your home? When do we get this sacramental? Why?

After the play: Why did the people honor Jesus? What type of Messiah were the people were expecting? What type of Messiah was Jesus? Why do we adore God?

CLASS PRAYER

Have the students sing a song acclaiming Christ as king. This could be a hymn sung on Passion Sunday such as "All Glory, Laud and Honor," "Blessings on the King," "Ride on, ride on," a "Holy, Holy" from the celebration of the Eucharist, or a general hymn of praise. Then pray a litany with the response "Have mercy on us." The students may add invocations.

Jesus, king of the ages,
Jesus, Son of David,
Jesus, the messiah foretold by the prophets,
Jesus, desire of the everlasting hills,
Jesus, king of glory,
Jesus, prince of peace,
Jesus, our savior,
Jesus, our redeemer,
Jesus, Son of God, …Amen.

The Entry Into Jerusalem

MATTHEW 21:1–11 MARK 11:1–11 LUKE 2:22–38 JOHN 12:12–19

(Jesus and Disciples enter. Bystander and colt are off to the side.)

Narrator   Jesus and his disciples walked toward Jerusalem.

Jesus   (to Disciples 1, 2) The two of you go into the village ahead of you. As you enter it, you will find a colt on which no one has ever sat. Untie it and bring it here. And if anyone should ask you, "Why are you untying it?" just say, "The master has need of it."

(Disciples 1, 2, walk toward colt. Jesus and other Disciples sit down.)

Disciple 1   There's the colt, just as Jesus said.

(Disciple 2 unties the colt.)

Bystander   What are you doing? Untying the colt?

Disciple 2   The master has need of it.

Bystander   Oh, all right then.

(Disciples 1, 2 and Bystander go to Jesus. Disciple 2 leads colt.)

Disciple 1   (to Jesus) We found it.

(Disciples throw cloaks over the colt. They help Jesus mount the colt. Crowd enters. Some throw cloaks on the ground. Others spread branches. Half the Crowd goes before Jesus, and half follows. He rides the colt.)

Disciples and Crowd   (loudly with joy) Hosanna to the Son of David! Blessed is he who comes in the name of the Lord! Hosanna in the highest!

Pharisee 1   (to Jesus) Teacher, stop them!

Jesus   I tell you, if they keep silent, the stones will shout out!

Narrator   The procession entered Jerusalem.

(Person enters.)

Person 1	Who is this?
Crowd	This is Jesus, the prophet from Nazareth in Galilee.
Pharisee 2	(to Pharisee 1) Look, the whole world is running after him!
Pharisee 1	(angrily) And we can do nothing.
Narrator	The crowd who praised Jesus on Palm Sunday a few days later was calling for his death. We are called to be faithful to Jesus every day, especially when it is hard.

The Paschal Mystery of Jesus

Leader's Guide

THE LAST SUPPER

Background Notes:

The earliest record of the institution of the Eucharist is in 1 Corinthians 11:23–25. In John's account of the Last Supper, the washing of the feet is described but not the institution of the Eucharist. The washing is a parable in action of what the Eucharist stands for. By assuming the role of the lowest, Jesus shows his disciples how they are to love one another. The four gospel accounts of the Last Supper differ in other details. In the gospels of Matthew and Mark, Judas's betrayal occurs before the Eucharist, but in Luke and John, Judas shares the meal with Jesus.

By the time of Jesus, the Jewish people had adapted the Hellenistic custom of eating while reclining on carpets and pillows around a low table. The diners shared large bowls in the center. It is supposed that the Last Supper was the Passover meal. Blessing of the bread and distributing it and the drinking of wine is part of that Jewish ritual. The paschal lamb is the symbol of Christ, the unblemished victim of the sin of humankind. As at the Passover meal, after sharing the bread and wine, Jesus, as presider, explains their meaning. Unlike at the Passover meal, the bread becomes his body and the wine, his blood. He is inaugurating a covenant. Just as covenants of the Old Testament were ratified by sprinkling the blood of the sacrificed animal over the people, Jesus seals his new covenant with his blood—the symbol of life. He is the new Passover victim.

Times for Use: Lessons on the Eucharist, service.

QUESTIONS FOR CHILDREN

Before the play: What is the greatest gift that anyone can give you? When did Jesus give us himself? When can we offer ourselves to God?

After the play: Why do we celebrate the Eucharist? What did Jesus ask of his disciples? How can we participate in the Eucharist fully? What are some special Masses you have celebrated?

CLASS PRAYER

Lord Jesus Christ, I firmly believe that you are present in this Blessed Sacrament as true God and true man, with your Body and Blood, soul and divinity. My redeemer and my judge, I adore your divine majesty together with the angels and saints. I believe, O Lord; increase my faith.

CAST	PROPS
Narrator	Table
Jesus	Bread
Twelve	Cup
Apostles	Bowl
	Robe for Jesus
	Basin
	Pitcher
	Towel
	Psalm to sing

The Last Supper

MATTHEW 26:20–30   MARK 14:17–26   LUKE 22:14–22   JOHN 13:1–27

(Jesus and Twelve Apostles are eating around table. John is next to Jesus.)

Narrator   At Jesus' direction the apostles had prepared for the Passover meal in a large upper room in Jerusalem. When it was evening, he came there with the Twelve.

(Jesus stands, removes his robe, and ties a towel around his waist. He pours water into a basin. He goes to each Apostle and "washes" and "dries" their feet. Peter is last.)

Peter   Master, are you going to wash my feet?

Jesus   You do not know now what I am doing, but later you will understand.

Peter   You will never wash my feet.

Jesus   Unless I wash you, you will have no share with me.

Peter   (extending hands) Master, then not only my feet, but also my hands and head.

(Jesus "washes" and "dries" Peter's feet. Then he puts on robe and goes to table.)

Jesus   Do you realize what I have done for you? You call me "teacher" and "master," and you are right, for that is what I am. So if I, the master and teacher, have washed your feet, you ought to wash one another's feet. Servants are not greater than their master. Amen, amen, I say to you, one of you will betray me.

(Apostles look at one another.)

John   Surely not I, Lord?

Apostles   Surely not I, Lord?

Jesus   It is the one to whom I hand the bread after I have dipped it.
(dips bread in a bowl and hands it to Judas) Do quickly what you are going to do.

(Judas exits. All continue eating.)

Jesus   (taking bread) Blessed are you, O Lord our God, King of the universe. You have made this bread holy. (breaks bread and passes it to Apostles) Take and eat. This is my body. Do this in remembrance of me.

(taking the cup) Blessed are you, O Lord our God, King of the universe, Creator of the vine. (gives cup to Apostles) Drink from it, all of you, for this is my blood of the covenant, which shall be shed for many for the forgiveness of sins.

I am with you only a little longer. I give you a new commandment, that you love one another. Just as I have loved you, you also should love one another. By this everyone will know that you are my disciples, if you have love for one another.

Peter   Lord, where are you going?

Jesus   Where I am going, you cannot follow me now.

Peter   (with enthusiasm) Lord, why can I not follow you now? I will lay down my life for you.

Jesus   Very truly, I tell you, before the cock crows you will have denied me three times.

(to all) Do not let your hearts be troubled. In my Father's house there are many dwelling places. If I go and prepare a place for you, I will come again and will take you to myself, so that where I am, there you may be also.

The Holy Spirit, whom the Father will send in my name, will teach you everything and remind you of all that I have said to you. I am going to the Father.

Rise, let us be on our way.

Narrator   Jesus gave us the gift of himself in the Eucharist. Each time we celebrate Mass we remember him and his sacrifice for us. We receive him into our hearts in Communion. Let us celebrate the Eucharist often and with great joy.

(All sing a psalm and exit.)

Leader's Guide

Background Notes:

The garden Jesus and his apostles go to was probably the private garden of a friend. Jesus takes the favored three and then leaves them to pray by himself. He is overwhelmed by sorrow. He asks that the Father take the cup of suffering away from him but submits to the divine plan. When he, the innocent one, takes on our sins and accepts the cup of suffering, we are saved.

People went to bed early in those days, and the apostles fall asleep in the garden instead of being a comfort to Jesus. They are a symbol of those who are not alert to their final test. When the Temple soldiers come to arrest Jesus and Peter tries to prevent them, Jesus stops him. It is the hour now for the climactic struggle between God and Satan.

The kiss of Judas is a normal Near East greeting. Here it serves to identify Jesus in the dark and becomes a symbol of betrayal.

Times for Use: Holy Week, with lessons on prayer, the mission of Jesus, obedience, the suffering of Jesus.

QUESTIONS FOR CHILDREN

Before the play: What emotions did Jesus have because he was human? When have you been afraid? What does it feel like? What can you do to help yourself when you are afraid?

After the play: How did Jesus show he was obedient to God? What happened because Jesus was willing to die for us? How can we be loyal to Jesus?

CLASS PRAYER

Invite the students to imagine they were there in the garden during the agony of Jesus:

In your mind's eye picture the dark garden and Jesus on his knees praying. Hear the insects and the breeze blowing through the olive leaves. Think of what must have gone through the mind of Jesus: his love for his Father and for us…his dread of the coming suffering and cruel death…the pain his suffering would cause his mother. [Pause.] Reflect on the ordeal Jesus was going through for you. [Pause.] Now place yourself in the scene next to him. What would you do? What would you say? [Allow time for silent reflection.]

CAST   PROPS

Narrator   Swords
Jesus
Eleven Apostles
Judas
Soldiers+
Malchus

The Agony in the Garden

MATTHEW 26:36–56 MARK 14:32–52 LUKE 22:39–53 JOHN 18:1–12

Narrator   After supper on Thursday evening, Jesus and the disciples went to the Mount of Olives. They stopped at the garden of Gethsemane.

(Jesus and Eleven Apostles enter.)

Jesus   Sit here while I go over there and pray. Peter, James, and John, come with me.

(Apostles sit. Jesus, Peter, James, and John walk over to side.)

Jesus   I am sorrowful even to death. Remain here and keep watch with me.

(Peter, James, and John sit. Jesus goes forward a little, kneels on the ground, and folds hands. Peter, James, and John close their eyes. Their heads nod.)

Jesus   My Father, if it is possible, let this cup pass from me. Yet, not what I want but what you want.

(Jesus rises and goes to Peter, James, and John.)

Jesus   (to Peter) So you could not stay awake with me for one hour? Watch and pray that you may not undergo the test. The spirit is willing, but the flesh is weak.

(Jesus goes forward, kneels, and prays. Peter, James, and John sleep again.)

Jesus   My Father, if it is not possible that this cup pass without my drinking it, your will be done.

(Jesus rises and goes to Peter, James, and John. He looks at them and shakes his head. He goes forward, kneels, and prays.)

Jesus   My Father, if it is not possible that this cup pass without my drinking it, your will be done.

(Jesus rises and goes to Peter, James, and John.)

Jesus   Are you still sleeping? The hour is come when the Son of Man is betrayed into the hands of sinners. Get up, let us go. See, my betrayer is at hand.

(Judas, Soldiers, and Malchus enter.)

Narrator   Judas had arranged with the soldiers that he would identify Jesus by kissing him.

Judas	(kissing Jesus) Greetings, Rabbi!
Jesus	Friend, do what you are here to do. (Soldiers grab Jesus. Peter draws a sword and swings at Malchus.)
Malchus	(screaming) Ahhh! My ear. (Jesus touches Malchus's ear.)
Malchus	(amazed) I'm healed!
Jesus	(to Peter) Put your sword back into its sheath. All who take the sword will perish by the sword. Do you think that I cannot call upon my Father and he will at once send me more than twelve legions of angels? (to Soldiers) Have you come out with swords and clubs to arrest me as though I were a robber? Day after day I sat teaching in the temple, yet you did not arrest me. But this is your hour, the time for the power of darkness. (Apostles exit, running. Soldiers walk Jesus out.)
Narrator	Jesus is our model in accepting God's will. When suffering comes into our lives, may we become stronger because of it and use it for good.

Leader's Guide

THE TRIAL BEFORE PILATE

Background Notes:

Jesus' trial before Pilate focuses on his innocence and on his identity. The dream of Pilate's wife and the hand-washing occur only in Matthew's account. These details underline the innocence of Jesus. The Scripture authors make the Jewish leaders, not Rome, responsible for the death of Jesus. The leaders bring Jesus to Pilate because they do not have the power to crucify. In choosing to free instead of Jesus the Zealot, the terrorist Barabbas (whose name means Son of the Father), they are choosing political liberation rather than the true Messiah.

Gospels portray Pilate as fickle and subservient to the Jewish crowd. History, on the other hand, tells us that Pilate was strong-willed and held the Jewish people in contempt. In the gospels, although Pilate finds Jesus without blame, he gives in to the pressure of the Jewish crowd when his career is threatened.

Jesus is presented by the evangelists as Messiah and king during the trial. The charge against him is that he said that he was king of the Jews. This claim amounts to treason against Rome, a capital offense. Jesus explains to Pilate that his kingdom is not of this world. In the end, the Roman soldiers mock him as king. They put a crown of thorns on him and a cloak, which is probably the scarlet cloak of the Roman soldiers. Ironically, these Gentiles unwittingly do homage to their real king as he is about to give his life for them and for all his people.

Scourging before crucifixion was routine procedure for the Romans. It was a terrible ordeal performed with a whip of leather strips ending in knots or bits of metal or bone. After this torture, Jesus is led to his throne, the cross.

Times for Use: Holy Week, with lessons on the identity of Jesus, the suffering of Jesus, the death of Jesus.

CAST	PROPS
Narrator	Cloak
Jesus	Crown of thorns
Pilate	Chair
Soldiers	Bowl
1, 2, 3, 4+	
Jewish	
Leaders 1, 2+	

QUESTIONS FOR CHILDREN

Before the play: When do you especially think about the suffering Jesus went through? How does his suffering give meaning to ours? What is a king? How is Jesus our king?

After the play: What sufferings did Jesus endure for us? Why did Pilate order Jesus crucified? What are the Stations of the Cross? How we can thank Jesus for being our Savior?

CLASS PRAYER

Soul of Christ, sanctify me.
Body of Christ, save me.
Blood of Christ, overwhelm me.
Water from the side of Christ, wash me.
Passion of Christ, strengthen me.
O good Jesus, hear me. Within your wounds shelter me. Permit me not to be separated from you. From the evil one protect me. At the hour of my death call me and bid me come to you, that I may praise you with all your saints for ever and ever. Amen.

The Trial Before Pilate

MARK 15:1–20 MATTHEW 27:11–31 LUKE 23:1–25 JOHN 18:28—19:16

(Pilate stands on one side of the stage with his back to the other. Soldiers stand in the background, arms crossed.)

Narrator On the morning after Jesus was arrested, soldiers brought him from Caiaphas, the high priest, to Pilate, the Roman procurator.

(Jesus and Jewish Leaders enter from opposite side. They stop some distance from Pilate.)

Jewish Leader 1 Pilate, we cannot enter your building, or we will not be able to eat the Passover meal.

(Pilate walks over to Jewish Leaders.)

Pilate What charge do you bring against this man?

Jewish Leader 2 If he were not a criminal, we would not have handed him over to you.

Pilate Take him yourselves and judge him according to your law.

Jewish Leader 1 We do not have the right to execute anyone.

(Pilate returns to his side of the stage. He turns to face the Jewish Leaders.)

Pilate (beckoning to Jesus) Come here.

(Jesus walks to Pilate.)

Pilate Are you the king of the Jews?

Jesus Do you ask this on your own or did others tell you about me?

Pilate I am not a Jew, am I? Your own nation and the chief priests handed you over to me. What have you done?

Jesus My kingdom is not of this world. If my kingdom were from this world, my followers would be fighting to keep me from being handed over to the Jews. But as it is, my kingdom is not from here.

Pilate	So you are a king?
Jesus	You say I am a king. For this I was born and for this I came into the world, to testify to the truth. Everyone who belongs to the truth listens to my voice.
Pilate	What is truth? (goes to Jewish Leaders) I find no guilt in him. But you have a custom that I release one prisoner to you at Passover. Do you want me to release to you Barabbas or Jesus, called Messiah? (Messenger enters and goes to Pilate.)
Messenger	Sir, your wife sends you a message. She says, "Have nothing to do with that righteous man. I have suffered much in a dream today because of him."
Pilate	(to Jewish Leaders) Which do you wish me to release to you, Barabbas or Jesus?
Jewish Leaders	Barabbas!
Pilate	(to Soldiers) Take him away and whip him. (Soldiers and Jesus exit.)
Narrator	The soldiers whipped Jesus. They wove a crown of thorns and placed it on his head. They clothed him in a purple cloak and mocked him saying, "Hail, king of the Jews." Then they returned him to Pilate. (Soldiers and Jesus enter. Pilate goes to Jewish Leaders.)
Pilate	Look I am bringing him out to you, so that you may know that I find no guilt in him. (Pilate motions for Jesus to come. Soldiers bring Jesus to Pilate. Pilate gestures toward Jesus.)
Pilate	Behold, the man!
Jewish Leaders	Crucify him. Crucify him.
Pilate	Take him yourselves and crucify him. I find no case against him.

Jewish Leaders	We have a law, and according to that law he ought to die, because he claimed to be the Son of God.
	(Pilate puts his hand to his face in fear and returns to his side of stage.)
Pilate	(to Jesus) Where are you from? (long pause) Do you not speak to me? Do you not know that I have power to release you and power to crucify you?
Jesus	You would have no power over me if it had not been given to you from above. For this reason the one who handed me over to you has the greater sin.
	(Pilate goes to Jewish Leaders.)
Pilate	This man should be released.
Jewish Leaders	If you release him, you are not a friend of Caesar. Everyone who makes himself a king sets himself against Caesar.
	(Pilate takes Jesus to chair and has him sit.)
Pilate	(to Jewish Leaders) Behold your king.
Jewish Leaders	We have no king but Caesar.
	(Pilate goes to bowl and washes his hands.)
Pilate	I am innocent of this man's blood. See to it yourselves.
Jewish Leaders	His blood be upon us and upon our children.
Pilate	(to Soldiers) Take him out and crucify him.
	(Soldiers go to Jesus and roughly pull him up. Soldiers and Jesus exit. Jewish Leaders cheer.)
Narrator	Jesus was condemned to death. By his suffering and death on the cross he saved the world. He saved you. What love and gratitude should fill our hearts when we recall this.

Leader's Guide

Background Notes:

No one witnessed the actual resurrection. The first clue that Jesus is risen is the empty tomb. All the gospels record that before dawn women came to the tomb. Although John focuses on Mary Magdalene (or Mary of Magdala), her use of "we" indicates that she was with others. John lets Peter enter the tomb first. Peter, therefore, predominates in the story. The apostles see the burial cloths. The wrapping for the head is rolled up and separate. This probably means that it was still in the oval shape it took when it was looped around the head and knotted at the top to keep the jaw from slacking. The presence of the linens discredits the rumor that the body was stolen. Thieves would not leave the wrappings behind. The disciples do not understand the full impact of the scene. They have yet to receive the Holy Spirit.

It is fitting that Mary Magdalene, who faithfully stood at the cross, is the first to see the risen Lord. But because he is so altered in his glorified state or because her vision is so blurred from tears, she mistakes him for the gardener. Her love for Jesus prompts her to ask where the body is so that she can take it. She is oblivious to whether or not she can do this. When Jesus says Mary's name, she recognizes him immediately. She calls him "Rabbouni," a form of rabbi. Jesus tells Mary to stop clinging to him. He still must return to the Father and complete the cycle of his glorification and our salvation.

Times for Use: Easter, with lessons on the Resurrection, women, Peter, love for Jesus.

QUESTIONS FOR CHILDREN

Before the play: What do we celebrate at Easter? How do you celebrate it at home? How do we know that Jesus rose from the dead?

After the play: How was Jesus the same and yet different after he rose?
How do you know that Mary Magdalene had deep love for Jesus? Why do you think John let Peter enter the tomb first? What difference does the resurrection make for us?

CLASS PRAYER

Invite the students to close their eyes and lead them to reflect on the consequences of Jesus' resurrection for us:

Because Jesus died and rose from the dead we too will have eternal life. Death is not the end for us. A whole new world awaits us. We will have glorified bodies with new life. St. Paul wrote that heaven is so wonderful that we can't even imagine what God has prepared there for us. Let us think for a moment what heaven will be like. There will be no more suffering, pain, and worry. We will be with God forever in perfect happiness. We will be with Mary and all the saints and angels in heaven. Many of the people we have loved on earth will be there too. We will see Jesus and be loved by him without end. Let us thank Jesus for making heaven possible for us. [Pause.] Now let's praise God for restoring to us the hope of everlasting life.

Sing an Easter song or an Alleluia.

CAST

Narrator
Jesus
Peter
John
Mary
Angels 1, 2

PROPS

Two cloths

The Resurrection

JOHN 20:1–18

(Peter and John are at the far side of the stage. Mary enters from the other side.)

Narrator	Early on the first day of the week, while it was still dark, Mary of Magdala came to the tomb, and saw the stone had been removed.

(Mary gasps and puts hands to face in horror. She runs to Peter and John.)

Mary	They have taken the Lord from the tomb, and we don't know where they have laid him.

(Peter and John run to the tomb. John arrives first and peers in the tomb. He waits for Peter. Peter arrives.)

John	I can see the burial cloths.
Peter	(stooping and going in tomb) Look. The cloth that covered his head is rolled up in a place by itself.

(John stoops and goes in tomb. Peter and John exit. Mary stands weeping. Angels 1, 2 enter and sit in the tomb.)

Angels 1, 2	Woman, why are you weeping?

(Jesus enters behind Mary.)

Mary	They have taken away my Lord, and I don't know where they laid him.

(Mary turns and sees Jesus.)

Jesus	Woman, why are you weeping? Whom are you looking for?
Narrator	Mary thought Jesus was the gardener.
Mary	(to Jesus) Sir, if you have carried him away, tell me where you laid him, and I will take him away.
Jesus	Mary!
Mary	(excitedly) Rabbouni! (kneels and clasps Jesus' knees)
Jesus	Do not hold onto me, because I have not yet ascended to the Father. Go to my

brothers and tell them I am going to my Father and your Father, to my God and your God.

(Mary rises and exits.)

Mary (shouting offstage) I have seen the Lord!

Narrator Because Jesus is alive, we can live forever. His rising brought us new life. All our actions ought to show that we are new people in Christ. They should shine forth Christ's love to everyone.

Leader's Guide

Background Notes:
The gospel accounts of the resurrection differ but all agree that Jesus' tomb was empty and that he appeared to various people. The women are going to anoint Jesus' body. As an afterthought, they wonder how they will move the heavy, flat stone that covers the entrance to the tomb. Their worries are allayed when they discover that the stone has already been moved for them. The women are full of fear on seeing the angel and the empty tomb. The details in this account of the resurrection highlight the glory of the event: the angel, the dazzling white clothes, the earthquake, the fainting guards. The disbelief of the disciples is understandable. In the gospels of Mark and Luke, Peter is singled out as the one who learns of the resurrection. Interestingly, it is women, not the apostles, who are the first heralds of the resurrection.

Times for Use: Easter, with lessons on the resurrection, women, Peter.

QUESTIONS FOR CHILDREN

Before the play: If someone told you that he was going to die and then rise from the dead, would you believe it? Why were there guards at Jesus' tomb?

After the play: In this account of the resurrection, what signs are there that it is a glorious event? Why didn't the disciples believe the good news at first? If we believe in the resurrection, how will we live?

CLASS PRAYER

Regina Caeli

Queen of heaven, rejoice, alleluia.
The Son whom you were made worthy to bear, alleluia,
Has risen as he said, alleluia.
Pray for us to God, alleluia.

Rejoice and be glad, O Virgin Mary, alleluia,
for the Lord has truly risen, alleluia.

Let us pray.

God of life,
you have given joy to the world
by the resurrection of your Son, our Lord Jesus Christ.
Through the prayers of his mother, the Virgin Mary,
bring us to the happiness of eternal life.
We ask this through Christ our Lord.
Amen.

CAST

Narrator
Angel
Mary
Women 1, 2
Guard+
Disciples 1, 2
Peter
Jesus

PROPS

Bags for spices
Chair for rock

The Appearance to the Women

MATTHEW 28:1–10 MARK 16:1–8 LUKE 24:1–12

(Stone is before tomb. Guards stand by it.)

Narrator   Very early when the sun had risen, on the first day of the week Mary of Magdala and other women went to the tomb. They brought spices to anoint Jesus.

(Mary and Women enter and walk toward tomb.)

Woman 1   Who will roll back the stone for us from the entrance to the tomb?

(Women shake.)

Woman 2   What was that?

Mary   An earthquake.

(Angel enters and rolls back stone. Guards fall to ground in a faint.)

Angel   (to Women) Do not be afraid! I know that you are looking for Jesus the crucified. He is not here (gestures to tomb) for he has been raised just as he said. Come and see the place where he lay. Then go quickly and tell his disciples, "He has been raised from the dead, and he is going before you to Galilee. There you will see him." This is my message for you.

(Women peer into tomb. They begin to run. Jesus enters and meets them.)

Jesus   Good morning!

Woman 1   (with joy) Jesus!

Woman 2   (excitedly) Master!

(Women kneel and bow to Jesus.)

Jesus   (laughing) Do not be afraid. Go tell my brothers to go to Galilee, and there they will see me.

(Jesus exits. Disciples enter. Women go to them.)

Woman 1   Jesus is alive!

Woman 2   He is risen.

Disciple 1   That's nonsense!

Woman 1   He spoke to us.

Disciple 2   You're out of your minds!

(Group stands arguing. Peter leaves group, goes to tomb, and peers in. He stands up amazed.)

Peter   The tomb is empty! How can this be?

Narrator   The risen Lord is alive in our world today. Be open to ways he comes to you and be ready to greet him.

Leader's Guide

Background Notes:
The Emmaus story is the story of all people who come to know Jesus. Two disciples are leaving Jerusalem with their hopes dashed. One is identified as Cleopas; the other could be his wife. They had hoped that Jesus was the Messiah but are discouraged by his death. When Jesus comes to them, not recognizing him, they summarize the good news for him. He dispels their confusion and doubts by explaining how the Scriptures foretell that the Messiah would have to suffer. Their hearts burn within them. When the travelers reach Emmaus, about seven miles from Jerusalem, the two disciples invite Jesus to stay with them. During supper as Jesus is breaking bread, they suddenly realize who he is. He vanishes, and they immediately return to Jerusalem to tell the other disciples what happened.

This account has the structure of the eucharistic liturgy. First the disciples hear the word, and then they share a meal with Christ. In the Eucharist, Jesus is present with his people no less than he was before his death. Our hearts too should burn within us.

Times for Use: Easter, with lessons on the resurrection, the identity of Jesus, the Eucharist.

QUESTIONS FOR CHILDREN

Before the play: Did you ever have the experience of not recognizing someone? Why didn't you recognize him or her? Why do you think some disciples wouldn't recognize Jesus after the resurrection?

After the play: Although Jesus died, he is present with us at the Eucharist. Why can he be present? In what ways is he with us? How can listening to God's word proclaimed at Mass bring us closer to Jesus? How does sharing the sacred bread and wine at Mass bring us closer to Jesus and one another?

CLASS PRAYER

Lord, in your sacrament we daily embrace you and receive you into our bodies. Make us worthy to experience the resurrection for which we hope. We have had your treasure hidden within us ever since we received baptismal grace. It grows ever richer at your sacramental table.
—St. Ephrem

CAST

Narrator
Jesus
Cleopas
Disciple

PROPS

Table
Three chairs
Bread

On the Emmaus Road

LUKE 24:13–35

Narrator   On the day of the resurrection two disciples were going to a village about seven miles from Jerusalem called Emmaus.

(Cleopas and Disciple enter.)

Cleopas   I can't believe he's dead.

Disciple   According to those women, he's not.

(Jesus enters and joins the Disciples.)

Jesus   What are you discussing as you walk along?

(Disciples stand still.)

Cleopas   (sadly) Are you the only visitor to Jerusalem who does not know of the things that have taken place there in these days?

Jesus   What things?

Disciple   The things that happened to Jesus the Nazarene, who was a prophet mighty in deed and word before God and all the people, how our chief priests and rulers handed him over to be condemned to death and crucified him.

Cleopas   But we had hoped that he was the one to redeem Israel. Yes, and besides all this, it is now the third day since these things took place.

Disciple   Moreover, some women from our group have astounded us. They were at the tomb early in the morning and did not find his body. They came back and told us that they had indeed seen a vision of angels who said that he was alive.

Cleopas   Then some of those with us went to the tomb and found it just as the women had described, but they did not see him.

Jesus   (shaking head) Oh, how foolish you are! How slow of heart to believe all that the prophets spoke! Was it not necessary that the Messiah should suffer these things and then enter into his glory? The Scriptures tell you this. Let me explain, beginning with Moses and the prophets.

(Jesus, Cleopas, and Disciple walk on, talking.)

Narrator	Jesus explained to them what referred to him in all the Scriptures until they approached the village.
	(Cleopas and Disciples stop. Jesus keeps walking.)
Cleopas	Stay with us.
Disciple	It is almost evening and the day is now nearly over.
Jesus	All right. I will.
	(Jesus smiles. He, Cleopas, and Disciple go to the table and sit.)
Jesus	(taking bread) Blessed are you, O Lord our God, King of the universe.
	(Jesus breaks the bread and passes it to Cleopas and Disciple.)
Cleopas and Disciple	(in awe) Jesus!
	(Jesus disappears backstage or under the table.)
Cleopas	He's gone!
Disciple	Weren't our hearts burning within us while he talked to us on the road and opened the Scriptures to us?
Cleopas	(excitedly) Let's go back to Jerusalem and tell the others what happened.
	(Cleopas and Disciple rise and run off.)
Narrator	The two disciples recognized Jesus in the breaking of the bread. At Mass we share the sacred bread and sacred wine. Our hearts should burn within us then, for Christ is present.

Leader's Guide

Background Notes:
The disciples experience the resurrected Jesus as a human being. He assures them he was not a ghost. He shows them his wounds, asks for food, and eats fish in front of them. Eating was an understood sign that someone was not a ghost. Jesus is able to eat just as the daughter of Jairus had been able to eat after Jesus raised her from the dead.

The disciples move from shock, confusion, and fear to peace and joy. Jesus recalls how he had told them about the closing events of his life on earth and how the Scriptures pointed to these events. He foretells that they will witness these things and preach repentance to all nations. It is the promised Spirit who will make things clear to the disciples and empower them to carry out their mission. In the Gospel of John, Jesus breathes on the apostles and gives them the Holy Spirit that day, enabling them to forgive sins.

Times for Use: Easter, with lessons on the resurrection, evangelization, the good news, ministry, eternal life.

QUESTIONS FOR CHILDREN

Before the play: How would you feel if the risen Lord appeared to you? Why might the apostles be afraid of Jesus after the resurrection? Why would Jesus visit them?

After the play: What could Jesus do because he had a glorified body? What were his first words to the apostles? How did Jesus identify himself? In what ways can we proclaim to others the good news that Jesus is risen? How will the Holy Spirit help us?

CLASS PRAYER

Lord, make me an instrument of your peace.
Where there is hatred, let me sow love;
where there is injury, pardon;
where there is doubt, faith;
where there is despair, hope;
where there is darkness, light;
where there is sadness, joy.

O Divine Master,
grant that I may not so much seek to be consoled, as to console;
to be understood, as to understand;
to be loved, as to love.
For it is in giving that we receive;
it is in pardoning that we are pardoned;
and it is in dying that we are born to eternal life.
—attributed to St. Francis of Assisi

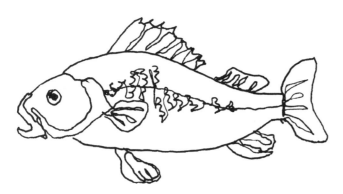

CAST

Narrator
Jesus
Disciples 1, 2+

PROPS

Table
Fish

The Appearance to the Apostles

LUKE 24:36–51

(Disciples are on stage, talking excitedly.)

Disciple 1 How amazing that he walked to Emmaus with those disciples.

Disciple 2 And they didn't know him until he broke bread!

(Jesus enters and stands in the middle of them.)

Jesus Peace be with you.

(Disciples gasp and shrink back, frightened.)

Jesus Why are you frightened? And why do doubts arise in your hearts? Look at my hands and my feet. See that it is I myself. Touch me and see, (extending hands) because a ghost does not have flesh and bones (gesturing to feet) as you can see I have.

(Disciples come forward with joy and amazement.)

Jesus Have you anything here to eat?

(Disciple 1 takes fish from table and gives it to Jesus.)

Jesus Thank you.

(Jesus "eats" the fish while the Disciples watch.)

Jesus These are my words that I spoke to you while I was still with you—that everything written about me in the law of Moses, the prophets, and the psalms must be fulfilled.
Thus it is written that the Messiah would suffer and rise from the dead on the third day and that repentance for the forgiveness of sins would be proclaimed in his name to all the nations, (makes a sweeping motion with arm) beginning from Jerusalem. (points down) You (points to Disciples) are witnesses of these things. And see, I am sending upon you what my Father promised, so stay in the city until you are clothed with power from on high.

Narrator After the resurrection Jesus did not scold the men who had deserted him. Instead he offered them peace. May we, like Jesus, be quick to forgive and forget.

109

Leader's Guide

Background Notes:

Jesus was truly resurrected. His entering through locked doors shows that he had not merely survived crucifixion. He had died and risen. He possesses new spiritual qualities. Jesus is, however, the same person the disciples knew and loved. The wounds in his hands and feet identify him. Jesus' first word to his disciples is "Shalom," that is, "Peace be with you." Understandably he had to calm their fears. Not only are the disciples seeing a person they knew had died, but someone almost all of them had abandoned.

Jesus' breathing on his disciples is a sign of the giving of his Spirit. Breath signifies life. The Spirit of creation brings us new life. Now that Jesus is risen, the Spirit will empower his church to carry on his mission. His disciples will share in his power to forgive and to reconcile the world through the sacraments. They, too, will bring peace.

Thomas, nicknamed "doubting Thomas," comes to believe that the Lord is risen not on the words of others but by his own eyes. He makes a great act of faith. He calls Jesus "Lord" and "God," terms that were used for the name of the God of Israel. Unlike Thomas' faith, our faith depends not on sight but on the gospel, the Word.

Times for Use: Easter, with lessons on the resurrection, forgiveness, faith, the Holy Spirit.

CAST

Narrator
Jesus
Disciples+
Thomas

QUESTIONS FOR CHILDREN

Before the play: What are some things you find hard to believe? Why do you believe them?

After the play: Why did the apostles need peace after the death and resurrection of Jesus? How we can make our faith grow stronger? Why did Jesus give us the sacrament of reconciliation?

CLASS PRAYER

Invite the students to contribute to a spontaneous litany of faith. Explain that someone will state a truth that we believe and then all will respond, "I believe. Jesus, increase my faith." Suggest thinking of the Apostles' Creed to get ideas. You might begin the prayer:

That God exists…
That Jesus loves me…
That I will live forever…

The Appearance to Thomas

(Disciples are on stage.)

Narrator   On the evening of the resurrection, the first day of the week, the disciples were behind locked doors in fear of the Jews.

(Jesus enters and stands in the middle of the Disciples. They step back in fear.)

Jesus   Peace be with you. It is really I, Jesus. See. (extends his hands) And see. (points to his side)

Disciple 1   Jesus, I'm so happy.

Disciple 2   We thought you were dead.

(Disciples laugh, clasp their hands together, and show joy.)

Jesus   Peace be with you. As the Father has sent me, so I send you. (breathes on the Disciples gently) Receive the Holy Spirit. Whose sins you forgive are forgiven them, and whose sins you retain are retained.

(Jesus exits. Thomas enters.)

Disciple 2   Thomas! You missed it.

Disciple 3   We have seen the Lord.

Thomas   (shaking head) Unless I see the mark of the nails in his hands (points to palms) and put my finger into the nailmarks and put my hand (holds up hand) into his side, I will not believe.

Narrator   A week later the disciples were again inside behind locked doors, and Thomas was with them.

(Jesus enters and stands among the Disciples.)

Jesus   Peace be with you. (to Thomas) Put your finger here (extending hands) and see my hands, and bring your hand and put it into my side, and do not be unbelieving, but believe.

Thomas   (kneeling) My Lord and my God!

Jesus   Have you believed because you have seen me? Blessed are those who have not seen and yet have come to believe.

Narrator   What we believe we take on faith. We have not seen God, or Jesus, or heaven. Our faith can grow stronger through prayer and study.

Leader's Guide

Background Notes:

As soon as Peter knows the Lord is on the shore, he dives into the water and swims to Jesus so that he would arrive faster than by boat. The Lord cooks breakfast, using some of the fish the disciples caught. After breakfast, the Lord establishes Peter's roles as shepherd and martyr. Peter had denied Jesus three times. Now Jesus gives him an opportunity to reverse the denial by a triple declaration of love. He commands Peter to show his love by assuming his own mission. He entrusts Peter with the care of his flock. Peter and his successors, the popes, are responsible for teaching, governing, and sanctifying the church.

When Jesus tells Peter he will stretch out his hands, he could be referring to Peter's being taken prisoner or being crucified. Peter was crucified under the emperor Nero. He kept the promise he made at the Last Supper that he would lay down his life for Jesus.

Today on the Sea of Galilee the Church of the Primacy stands on the site where it is believed Jesus commanded Peter to lead his church.

Times for Use: Lessons on the church, Peter, the pope.

QUESTIONS FOR CHILDREN

Before the play: How does the pope show that he loves Jesus? How do you show love for Jesus?

After the play: What role did Peter have in the early church? What were his strengths and weaknesses? How do we show love and respect for the Holy Father?

CLASS PRAYER

Holy Spirit, guide the leaders of our church: our Holy Father and bishops. Give them wisdom to make right decisions. Give them compassion to be good shepherds. Give them courage to stand up for what is right. Give them zeal in proclaiming the Gospel and the kingdom of God. Make them one as they lead us to the glory of God the Father. Above all, fill their hearts with love so that they truly may be Christ for the world. Amen.

CAST | PROPS

CAST	PROPS
Narrator	Wood for fire
Jesus	
Peter	
Thomas	
Nathanael	
James	
John	
Apostle 1	
Apostle 2	

Jesus and Peter

(Jesus, Peter, Thomas, Nathanael, James, John, Apostle 1, and Apostle 2are seated in a semicircle around wood.)

Narrator The third time Jesus appeared to the apostles after the Resurrection, they were fishing. Although they had caught nothing all night, Jesus helped them catch many fish. When Peter realized that it was Jesus on the shore, he dove into the water and swam to him. There Jesus served the apostles breakfast.

Thomas That was delicious. I was starved. Thank you.

Apostles Yes, thank you.

Jesus My pleasure. (turning to Peter) Simon, son of John, do you love me more than these?

Peter Yes, Lord. You know that I love you.

Jesus Tend my lambs. (pause) Simon, son of John, do you love me?

Peter Yes, Lord. You know that I love you.

Jesus Tend my sheep. (pause) Simon, son of John, do you love me?

Peter (exasperated) Lord, you know everything. You know that I love you.

Jesus Feed my sheep. Very truly, I tell you, when you were younger, you used to fasten your own belt and to go wherever you wished. But when you grow old, you will stretch out your hands, (extend hands) and someone else will fasten a belt around you and take you where you do not wish to go. Follow me.

Peter (pointing to John) Lord, what about him?

Jesus If it is my will that he remain until I come, what is that to you? Follow me!

Narrator Peter did feed Jesus' sheep. He became the chief shepherd of Christ's church. And as Jesus foretold in this story, Peter was crucified for his faith in Jesus. May our love for Jesus make us ready to give everything for him, even our lives.

Leader's Guide

Background Notes:

The ascension is a part of the paschal mystery. In Matthew, Mark, and Luke the ascension takes place on the day of the resurrection, but in the Acts of the Apostles it occurs forty days after the resurrection.

The story of the ascension foreshadows the parousia (second coming). Jesus appears and on a mountain is exalted, or taken up into glory. The cloud is a symbol of divine presence as it was during the Exodus and the Transfiguration. Jesus is seated at the right hand of the Father. Jesus has authority from God and power over the whole universe. Jesus' ascension is the assurance that someday we too will be taken up into glory.

At the ascension Jesus gives "the great commission" to the eleven apostles. They are to be his personal witnesses and to make disciples of all people, Jewish people as well as Gentiles. Jesus promises to still be Emmanuel, God with us. He blesses the apostles. It is while they are there in an attitude of worship that they are ordered to go and take the good news to all. Angels explain that Jesus would return the same way they saw him go, referring to the final judgment day.

On the top of Mount Olivet in Jerusalem today there is a Shrine of the Ascension. Inside is a rock in the ground that, according to tradition, is where Jesus ascended.

Times for Use: Before the Ascension, with lessons on evangelization, the Holy Spirit.

QUESTIONS FOR CHILDREN

Before the play: Where is Jesus now? Who carries on his work for him? How does Jesus help them?

After the play: Why is the ascension such a great feast that it is a holy day of obligation? What did Jesus commission the apostles to do? How did they carry out their commission? Who is called to witness to Jesus today? How can you do this?

CLASS PRAYER

O Lord, teach me to be generous.
Teach me to serve you as you deserve;
to give and not to count the cost;
to fight and not to deed the wound;
to toil and not to seek for rest;
to labor and not to ask for reward
save that of knowing that I am doing your holy will.
Amen.

CAST   PROPS

Narrator   **Large paper cloud**
Jesus
Disciples+
Man 1
Man 2

The Ascension

MATTHEW 28:16–20   MARK 16:15–20   LUKE 24:50–53   ACTS OF THE APOSTLES 1:6–11

Narrator   The eleven disciples went to Mount Olivet as Jesus had directed them.

Disciple 1   Lord, is this the time when you will restore the kingdom to Israel?

Jesus   It is not for you to know the times or periods that the Father has set by his own authority. But you will receive power when the Holy Spirit has come upon you. And you will be my witnesses in Jerusalem, in all Judea and Samaria, and to the ends of the earth. (makes sweeping motion with arm)
All authority in heaven and on earth has been given to me. Go therefore (points to distance) and make disciples of all nations, baptizing them in the name of the Father and of the Son and of the Holy Spirit, and teaching them to obey everything that I have commanded you. And remember, I am with you always, to the end of the age.

Narrator   As the men were watching, Jesus was lifted up, and a cloud took him out of their sight.

(Jesus raises hands over the apostles in blessing. He backs off, and a cloud covers him.)

(Man 1 and Man 2 enter.)

Man 1   Men of Galilee, why do you stand looking up toward heaven?

Man 2   This Jesus, who has been taken up from you into heaven, will come in the same way as you saw him go into heaven.

Narrator   The apostles returned to Jerusalem where they stayed in an upper room, praying and awaiting the Holy Spirit. We, who have received the Holy Spirit at Baptism, have the power to witness to Jesus. Let us do this in our words and actions.

(Disciples exit.)

Sunday and Feastday Gospels
that Correspond to the Plays in this book

LITURGY	EVENT
Second Sunday of Advent A, B, C	The Baptism of Jesus (John the Baptist)
Third Sunday of Advent B	The Baptism of Jesus
Third Sunday of Advent C	The Baptism of Jesus
Fourth Sunday of Advent B	The Annunciation
Fourth Sunday of Advent C	The Visitation
Christmas Mass at Midnight A, B, C	The Birth of Jesus
Christmas Mass at Dawn A, B, C	The Birth of Jesus
January 1, Octave of Christmas, Solemnity of Mary, Mother of God	The Birth of Jesus
Sunday in the Octave of Christmas B	The Presentation
Sunday in the Octave of Christmas C	The Boy Jesus in the Temple
Epiphany A, B, C	The Visit of the Magi
Sunday after January 6 A, B, C	The Baptism of Jesus
First Sunday of Lent A, B, C	The Temptation of Jesus
Second Sunday of Lent A, B, C	The Transfiguration of Jesus
Third Sunday of Lent A	The Samaritan Woman
Third Sunday of Lent B	The Cleansing of the Temple
Fourth Sunday of Lent B	Nicodemus
Fifth Sunday of Lent C	The Woman Caught in Adultery
Passion Sunday (Procession) A, B, C	The Entry into Jerusalem
Passion Sunday A, B, C	The Last Supper
	The Agony in the Garden
	The Trial before Pilate
Passion Sunday B	The Anointing at Bethany
Holy Thursday (Chrism Mass) A, B, C	Rejection at Nazareth
Holy Thursday A, B, C	The Last Supper (Washing of the Feet)
Good Friday A, B, C	The Trial before Pilate
Easter Vigil A, B, C	The Appearance to the Women

Sunday and Feastday Gospels
that Correspond to the Plays in this book

LITURGY	EVENT
Easter Sunday A, B, C	The Resurrection
Second Sunday of Easter A, B, C	The Appearance to Thomas
Third Sunday of Easter A	On the Emmaus Road
Third Sunday of Easter B	The Appearance to the Apostles
Third Sunday of Easter C	Jesus and Peter
Fifth Sunday of Easter A, C	The Last Supper
Sixth Sunday of Easter A, B, C	The Last Supper
Ascension A, B, C	The Ascension
Pentecost A, B, C	The Appearance to the Apostles
Trinity Sunday A	Nicodemus
Trinity Sunday B	The Ascension
Second Sunday of the Year B	The First Apostles
Third Sunday of the Year B	The Call of the First Apostles
Third Sunday of the Year C	Rejection at Nazareth
Fourth Sunday of the Year C	Rejection at Nazareth
Tenth Sunday of the Year A	The Call of Matthew
Eleventh Sunday of the Year C	The Pardon of the Sinful Woman
Twelfth Sunday of the Year C	Peter's Profession of Faith
Fourteenth Sunday of the Year B	Rejection at Nazareth
Sixteenth Sunday of the Year C	Martha and Mary
Twenty-First Sunday of the Year A	Peter's Profession of Faith
Twenty-Fourth Sunday of the Year B	Peter's Profession of Faith
Twenty-Seventh Sunday of the Year B	The Blessing of the Children
Twenty-Eighth Sunday of the Year B	The Rich Young Man
Twenty-Ninth Sunday of the Year A	Paying Taxes to Caesar
Thirty-First Sunday of the Year C	Zacchaeus, the Tax Collector
Thirty-Second Sunday of the Year B	The Widow's Offering

Index of Themes

The following topics can be enlivened by a playlet in this book.

Index of Themes

The following topics can be enlivened by a playlet in this book.

Index of Themes

The following topics can be enlivened by a playlet in this book.